TOWARD CAMDEN

Black Outdoors / Innovations in
the Poetics of Study / *A series edited by*
J. Kameron Carter & Sarah Jane Cervenak

Toward

Camden

Mercy Romero

Duke University Press / *Durham & London* / 2021

Printed in the United States of America on acid-free paper ∞
Designed by Aimee C. Harrison
Typeset in Portrait Text, Canela Text, and Univers LT Std
by Copperline Book Services

Library of Congress Cataloging-in-Publication Data
Names: Romero, Mercy, [date] author.
Title: Toward Camden / Mercy Romero.
Other titles: Black outdoors.
Description: Durham: Duke University Press, 2021. | Series: Black
outdoors | Includes bibliographical references and index.
Identifiers: LCCN 2020056098 (print)
LCCN 2020056099 (ebook)
ISBN 9781478013785 (hardcover)
ISBN 9781478014706 (paperback)
ISBN 9781478022008 (ebook)
Subjects: LCSH: Community development—New Jersey—Camden. |
Hispanic Americans—New Jersey—Camden—Social conditions. |
African Americans—New Jersey—Camden—Social conditions. |
Camden (N.J.)—Social conditions—20th century. | Camden (N.J.)—
Social life and customs—20th century. | Camden (N.J.)—Economic
conditions—20th century. | BISAC: SOCIAL SCIENCE / Sociology /
Urban | SOCIAL SCIENCE / Ethnic Studies / American / Hispanic
American Studies
Classification: LCC HN80. C32 R66 2021 (print) |
LCC HN80. C32 (ebook) | DDC 307.1/40974987—dc23
LC record available at https://lccn.loc.gov/2020056098
LC ebook record available at https://lccn.loc.gov/2020056099

Publication of this book is supported by Duke University Press's
Scholars of Color First Book Fund.

Cover art: Xaviera Simmons, *Appear, Appease, Applaud (Also, Perhaps, Maybe)*, 2008. Courtesy the artist and David Castillo Gallery.

CONTENTS

ACKNOWLEDGMENTS

/

I am grateful for the professors I met in California, especially José David Saldivar, Patricia Hilden, Carlos Muñoz, Saidiya Hartman, Norma Alarcón, and Gina Dent. I hope this book is in some way a tribute to how much I learned from, appreciate, and admire each of them. Alfred Arteaga was my professor and a dear friend. I miss him very much, the sound of his voice, and the ease of our friendship. Being a graduate student in Ethnic Studies at the University of California, Berkeley enriched my experience. I am grateful to the graduate students I got to learn alongside, and for all the people in this community who showed me so much kindness. Thank you.

I began to consider this book many years ago in an Ethnic Studies seminar with Professor Patricia Hilden, when she asked us to think for a bit about the question, Where is home? Since then I have been fortunate to travel to many places and share this writing. I am very grateful to the folks with whom I shared each of these academic spaces, and for the many questions that pushed me to think differently and further.

I feel very lucky to have life experiences and memories that begin, for now, in Camden. My mother and father are central to how I have imagined and approached this writing. My mother told me to "love the learning" when I was so nervous about leaving Camden to study elsewhere.

She breathed new life into me that night. This book is dedicated to her, with all my love. Thank you for being my first and best teacher, for loving me as I am, and for so much laughter. I'm also shaped by my love for my father and his love for me, especially when I have been sick. I hope this book holds some part of what that love has meant for my understanding. Thank you for trusting me. Thank you for reading and loving Walt Whitman and James Baldwin and for passing this love to me. That I can turn to you both, even still, means the world to me. My three sisters and their families hosted, fed, loved, and encouraged me when I was out running around Camden, returning from the loneliness and confusion of an empty and boarded up house or trying to sort out a language to understand what was happening and write this book. I am thankful that parts of me come from my sisters and that we come from the same place. Thank you, M. J. P., for being the love in my life for a long time. I love you. I am grateful to you and your family, especially your mom, whose love and care for our kids made it possible for me to go to work and not worry. I'm grateful for my family, and lately I've been thinking a lot about my grandparents. Their migration stories and the places that made them—Morovis, Barranquitas, Adjuntas, Jayuya, Ponce, Lorain, Bridgeport, and Camden—turn and sound in my imagination and extend what this book has taught me. Thanks to my beautiful and brilliant children who have been with me as I've written this book. You showed me the waves, the lightning, and the clear path; I am ever grateful for your camaraderie and love. May you know the full blessings of the Puerto Rican and African American dreamers who made you, and may you be in service to that vision.

I am so grateful for the many friendships made in Camden, New York, and the Bay Area. All of the wonderful friends I have known accompany me, and through their examples they help me to have courage. That they have my back is the spirit that opens the first chapter of this book. Thanks to my colleagues for hiring me and for creating a place and a way to work that brings me growth and happiness. Thanks to my students who work so very hard and make the classroom vibrate and matter. Thanks to Camden's students, who inspired me from day one and who are a blessing to the city and the world. Thanks to Ryan Kendall, Susan Albury, Aimee Harrison, and the people at Duke University Press for publishing this book, and to the anonymous readers who helped to usher it into print with so much kindness and generosity. Thank you, Ken Wissoker, for your steady presence, patience, warmth of heart, and encouragement. Thank you, Paula Durbin-Westby, for your work on the index. Thank you, Camilo José Vergara, for allowing me to use your photograph in this book. Thank you, Xaviera Simmons, for allowing me to use your photograph as the cover art of this book. Thank you, Fred Moten, for the thoughtfulness that serves as an epigraph to chapter 1. Thank you, reader.

PROLOGUE

/

When I was eighteen or so I got to hear the poet Martín Espada read. I went to the reading with another girl. We were new friends. As we crossed Broadway, the distance between Barnard and Columbia, I listened to her talk about where she was from, one of her many stories about the beautiful Bay Area city that was the source of her father's blues and her mother's kind of love. The poetry reading must have meant a lot to us that evening and there must have been a special discount (maybe a two-for-one) because, as poor as we were, we each bought a book. She got *Rebellion Is the Circle of a Lover's Hands*, and I, *City of Coughing and Dead Radiators*. We waited in line so Espada could inscribe them, bless us with a few more words. A few years later when she left New York, her son in her arms, she gifted me her copy. (You can only take so much when you move.) Where are those books now? They may be down to the rot of our Camden basement, or hiding out in a Rubbermaid somewhere in my sister's storage container.

That evening, Martín Espada prefaced his reading of his poem "Who Burns for the Perfection of Paper" with a story. Once, when he was a law student, he held a legal pad, the long yellow pages made less unruly because they are bound at the top. And he remembered his own teenage hands working the paper edges of what would become the bundle. When he was sixteen he had worked at a factory where they made legal pads.

Glue secured it all, but it made his paper cuts burn and shout. Now he dwelled in thought, of the assembly, the cuts, and the paperwork.

But maybe after all he didn't preface his poem with a story? Maybe it was just the poem. Either way, I remember it this way. I remember it twice and in two voices, or between story and poetry.

I think of the story now. It is a couple of hours before sunrise. My boyfriend is asleep next to me. I asked this prologue to come. I asked yesterday. Make me ready to write tomorrow, I said, almost aloud. I stood at the kitchen window above a clean sink, my own children dealing in their evening homework, notebooks, and math facts, and I almost prayed it.

A Pair of Hands Upturned and Burning

Puerto Rican rallies mother, father, poet, writer, abuelita, grandfather, cousin, friend, titi, tio, sister, brother, daughter, you, beloved, son, neighbor, self, singer, nobody, me, and so on. You can shout, whisper, sing, draw out, or spit out some of these words when you read this list aloud. This may be how it is chosen, how it is made in relation, how it agitates against loss, is lost, or is what endures.

We arrived in Camden a handful of years after the 1971 riot, and after most of the storefronts in our neighborhood were permanently closed to us, hung in what would seem like an eternity of wooden boards and nails. My father trailed his brother, mother, and sisters. Eventually they all moved away, but we stayed on. I suppose we watched as houses vanished too, first behind the telltale of wood and neighborhood tags, then in fire, smoke, or wrecking ball. I grew to wonder about what remains, the left-behind and haphazard shapes on a landscape, like empty lots and vacants, and what might be pictured at and below the boards, all indications of life or life signs.

In the late summer of 1971 Puerto Rican people in Camden, New Jersey, rallied when police beat a Puerto Rican man. Over the course of three August days, people took to each other to grieve and protest in Camden. The Puerto Rican man had been pulled over by two Camden police officers. They beat him brutally and murderously, because afterward he was put on life support. He was reported to be in a coma and internally poisoned by his own ruptured small bowel.[1] When his life signs waned, his family's attorney (a man called Poplar) received a call from Camden's Mayor, Joseph Nardi: "He's not dead, but everyone figured that in order not to throw fuel on the fire, we didn't want him dead." Poplar convinced the Puerto Rican man's wife to keep him on life support.[2]

The Puerto Rican man's death was put on hold. He was kept on life support in the hospital in order to abate what the city's leaders imagined as an impending riot. Such was the administrative attempt to slow his death and control the movement and narrative of Camden's insurgent Puerto Rican political histories of 1971, which would constellate with other antiracist and anticarceral rebellions across the country.[3]

> He's not dead,
> but everyone figured that
> in order not to throw fuel on the fire
> we didn't want him dead.

I find this statement in an online newspaper archive. I sat with the phrasing for some time, a long time, troubled. I think of a part of Rick Barot's poem "Tarp," when he writes:

> There is no tarp for that raging figure in the mind
> that sits in a corner and shreds receipts
> and newspapers. There is no tarp for dread,
> whose only recourse is language
> so approximate it hardly means what it
> means:
> He is not here. She is sick. She cannot remember
> her name. He is old. He is ashamed.[4]

What does it mean to be pushed through accounting? To be figured as fuel and fire? To become a remainder.

On either end of this equation is a "not" death, a want of not dead: "He's not dead . . . we didn't want him dead."

This is the administration of life and the logic of population control. It is the other side of care for Puerto Ricans (in Camden), an administrative figuration of need, and the order of our dispossession and disappearance there.[5]

It may then have been unthinkable to say instead, "We wanted him to live." The Puerto Rican man who was beaten on July 30, 1971, and kept on life support through August 20 and reported dead on September 15 is called by two names in newspaper reports: Rafael Rodriguez and Horacio Jimenez. It is said that he gave the police a different name, a false name.

The line between Rafael/Horacio holds this tension, gestures perhaps toward how he tried to pass, cut, and slip interrogation, rally—all that he was up against—before he was finally allowed to die. For me, that slip continues to resonate and disturb the scene.

Rafael/Horacio was forty when he was killed. He had been driving through Camden, coming back home for a visit, it is said, because he had moved, lived elsewhere. Newspapers from that time describe the ensuing three or four days of rebellion and fires in the city that followed the breakdown in talks between the mayor and Puerto Rican community leaders and Rafael/Horacio's death. Camden structures, homes, businesses, gathering spots, and vacants were burned. Hundreds of people were arrested, and this rebellion was, like Rafael/Horacio, called by at least two names: the Camden Riots and the Puerto Rican Riots.[6]

A 2011 *Courier Post* newspaper retrospective on those four days includes the voices of Camden residents who were present at City Hall during the first rally against police brutality. The article describes a scene conjured by a man named Delgado, whose memory of that night reaches toward the making of an energy and a peoplehood, somewhere between a nowhere and a here: "'I remember that night, the people got energy from nowhere. . . . These parking meters here, we pulled them up out of the ground. That's how mad we were.' K-9 dogs and police in riot gear filtered out of the building. The mob overturned police cars and shattered windows. 'People can only take so much,' Delgado said. 'That was the last straw for Camden.' 'The people of Camden went to city hall to demonstrate,' he said. 'They wanted justice. Nardi said he had no time for the people, [but the] people wanted to say something.'"

Shared feelings crowd and collect. They accompany, want, extend, and claim. They may pass for other things—wanting to "say something" may look like the mad pulling of a parking meter right up out of the ground, the shattering of a window for what cannot be recovered. Delgado's repetition of "the people" of Camden pulls away from the reportage's characterization of a mob. It is the police who are in "riot gear," a tactical performance that sets the stage for and anticipates violence. The reportage turns away from Delgado and narrates the scene of a riot, as cops filter out of a building and the people become a mob, pulling and overturning a landscape. Yet what does Delgado mean when he says, "the people got energy from nowhere"? What is the generative promise and spatial power of and to the people? If nowhere is a site of energy, then the recollection's turn toward this landscape may indicate another generation, a making at work. In this landscape a wrested parking meter is an uprooted signpost; what was designated as a point of arrival becomes the sign of a moving target (get back in your car), as the driver is accosted, is beaten, and dies, in transit, both in and away from home, toward Camden. The article narrates a Puerto Rican man who was off work that day and who was from Camden. He is returning to the city, driving around on his day off. In the media rendition of those hot, humid, and rainy days that stretched between July 31 and August 21 is an imagined transparency of possible events (the will to riot, the will to destroy), not toward a collective movement and an always in relation, but at a downfall, an unbecoming of a people and a place. An excerpt of a statement released by the city's director of public safety at the time launches an attack against Camden's Puerto Ricans and is totally laden with this vision of unbecoming, of absolute downfall: "The ruthless, despicable, cowardly and shameful conduct attributed to that animalistic group of rationless two-legged beasts could only be surpassed in nature and degree by the two-faced appalling actions as represented by the representative negotiators busily disgracing their name and culture while their cohorts unleashed their fury against an unwilling police contingent situated at the scene."[7]

Camden's Mayor Nardi imposed a state of emergency that closed the city and imposed a curfew to restrict outdoor movements between 8:00 p.m. and 7:00 a.m. Routes into the city were closed. Alcohol and gasoline sales were suspended, as they, too, were imagined as "fueling" the collective body. The curfew that closed the city was also an act of (preemptive) mass criminalization thinly disguised as care and protection. Curfew shut folks inside and deprived them of the consolation of each other and their many forms of nighttime movements. The curfew attempted to stop for three consecutive days any reunion with the cover of night, that which necessitates and makes home for all forms of life and strides. The curfew attempted to still Camden's community force, the many Puerto Rican and African American people who worked regularly and il/legibly both with and against the prevailing democratic order to effect change in their communities, to push and shift the world.[8] Of course, people did not obey: "'The whole problem lies with the mayor,' Mario Rodriguez, former Camden City councilman who now is a commissioner for the

State Division of Civil Rights, claimed. 'He kept those people waiting for 10 hours. He kept them waiting in the heat and in the rain. He avoided sitting down with them.'"[9]

Sometimes in the Camden summertime it is finally cool enough to be outside at nightfall. Sitting outdoors with the shapes of trees and things, or at the threshold of a porch, your bit of sky may be wrapped in trees and the sounds of a neighborhood breathing together, however quickly. What comfort in that necessary night walk, even if it's just to the end of the block or around the corner, the air outside against the full heat of the indoors. No air conditioner. Broken back doors nailed shut, all the downstairs windows barred—you've got to get outside. To think, act, and move. Just here and just in this way. If the solution and grieving come this way, at the electric charge of activity, movement, stroll, pull, and run, and if it can arrive in place, in that movement between you and this ground and piece of atmosphere, at that corner, between these houses, that generative public where we leave a bit of ourselves and our mark for the next one who comes along. When all of nature isn't the "property of man," but rather the space where we come to be, walk, and think as a part of it all.[10] To exist this way at a state of emergency, against curfew and isolation, against the nightly transformations of an entire city into a jail or prison cell, is kind of impossible. At the state of emergency, the coming night itself inaugurates an open-air prison, a controlled atmosphere. At the logic of the curfew, all of Camden's skies were bullet ridden, lit up by smoke and fire, and so all of the night and its seasonal and cyclical choreographies were suspended. It amounted to people being kept apart when they really needed to be together, and the only place where we can all be together is outside.

Who Burns for the Perfection of Paper

The Walt Whitman House in Camden did not burn that summer. Not necessarily because people wanted to spare Whitman's old house or honor the poet's legacy (in the city), but rather because the curator at the time, Eleanor Ray, an African American woman who grew up right next door, came outside and told people to keep it moving. In this way, she is said to have held off the fires and ushered along the people outdoors.[11] Ray's thirty-five-year tenure at the Walt Whitman House started in 1955 and she was told, "Because the neighborhood (located just south of Broadway) was changing, they wanted a Black person to be custodian."[12] Ray began to see the house as "an extension of me." Reports of Ray's presence outdoors that August of 1971 describe her as protective, both sitting on the porch and sitting on the porch with a broom. The three days of rebellion are called a "rampage," "tide," "disorders": "When Puerto Ricans and blacks went on a rampage here last August, Mrs. Eleanor Ray sat protectively on the stoop of poet of democracy Walt Whitman's old home. The disorders, in protest against the alleged beating by two policemen of a Puerto Rican—he later died—led to about a million dollars' worth of damage. The tide came to within two doors of the Whitman house at 330 Mickle Boulevard before receding."[13]

In another article about the uprising, Eleanor Ray is pictured seated outside on the steps with a broomstick held across her lap. The caption reads, "A Broomstick against a Riot . . . Custodian Protected Walt Whitman's Home." Her body faces the camera, but she peers off to the side and into the distance, as if she is watching someone outside the frame. She holds the broom like a shotgun across her lap, but also like someone who is going to sweep the stoop. It strikes me that this hold is the same, and I rethink what she might have meant when she said this house is "an extension of me." Five years earlier, in 1966, Ray remarked that the house had hosted just three visitors one week and none the next: "Not many people know about the home and it's been so hot. . . ."[14] She posits the heat as keeping people at bay.

From inside this little house, Walt Whitman would often ask, or his friend and interlocutor Horace Traubel would ask him, after the weather. The heat. Traubel described August 23, 1891, this way: "Spent about five minutes with W. Sultriest day of the year. The whole community a growl."[15] Whitman asks Traubel whether it is as hot in Philadelphia as it is in Camden. Horace says yes, maybe even hotter. Traubel describes Whitman as fanning himself, passing a whole day sitting and fanning and dozing in the heat of his bedroom. Those days Whitman kept his bedroom windows mostly closed or only partially open. Whitman remarks that he likes ventilation. Their different perspectives on how open a window must be to be "open" and to circulate the air is amusing.[16] I wonder whether Whitman's mess, his piles of papers and things scattered around the floor, were part of the reason he kept just one window open.[17] Imagine the papers flying around the room in a gust or the rains coming in. He couldn't walk very well by this time. He was old and infirm, and too much of the wind may have moved his stuff around more than he liked or perhaps chilled him more than he liked. Whitman had been a walker. Sometimes it seems as if *Leaves of Grass* is a walk.[18] Of the heat, Whitman complained often, and yet he said too: "But this cool weather don't entirely satisfy me. It is important for my best condition that the pores should be kept open—that I should exude freely—throw off—shake away—have good operations of the skin. And I find I do not, as the days get cool. The heat brought its own troubles, I know—I was feeble under it—it sapped me of some strength—but after all gave me a sense of liberty."[19]

That this heat should be in Camden, where he felt free and was open at the pores, delights me and also helps me to understand summertime nights and (body) heat in Camden and what liberty means in Camden: to "exude freely" and to feel "feeble" and "sapped." When Camden is made at its African American and Puerto Rican histories and Black freedom movements, that is, to exude freely, to throw off, to shake away—like the fights for just housing for the poor, for a life, and against police brutality. At political protests that wrest property from land/scape and the riotous energy and sociality of a gathering is the energy and peoplehood of sapped, feeble, and willing bodies, a collective sensing its liberty.

To deal with the heat, Whitman often assumed different positions and states of dress, seated just at the top of the stairs or by a window or with head in hands. He asked his friend Horace about the meaning of heat one evening: "W. in his room—not reading—thought the light was up—head resting on hands, elbow on arm of the chair. Room hot—air pretty bad—he conscious of it, said, 'This heat today—what does it mean? It seems to me as bad a spell as any yet.' But he keeps two windows out of three closed, which is one cause of the oppressive air."[20]

Whitman asks, "This heat today—what does it mean?" Perhaps he was referring to a quality, a kind of thought or meaning made in that heat. What does heat mean? What does summertime heat in Camden mean? On August 25, 1891, two days after Traubel described the Camden heat and the whole community as a "growl," Whitman and Traubel overheard a Black person laughing just outside Whitman's window:

We heard the hearty laugh of a negro out on the street. Warrie remarked, "I do believe the niggers are the happiest people on the earth." W. saying at once, "That's because they're so damned vacant." I laughingly interposed, "That would be a bad thing to tell an anti-slavery man." He taking it up in this way, "It would—it was a bad thing. But I used to say it, though it always raised a storm. That was one of the points on which O'Connor and I always agreed. Charles Eldridge, however, *not*. That the horror of slavery was not in what it did for the nigger but in what it produced of the whites. For we quite clearly saw that the white South, if the thing continued, would go to the devil— could not save themselves. What slaveholding people can? Not, of course, because I could be cruel to the nigger or to any of the animals— to a horse, dog, cat, anything—especially *me*—for my dear daddy was remarkable everywhere he went for his kindness to the dumb beasts. A fine trait I hope I inherited—which I believe I did."[21]

Like the public safety officer whose 1971 statement likens Camden's Puerto Ricans to "two-legged beasts," Whitman overhears, storms, and corrals the sounds of free Black life in an awful taxonomy set to realign self-making freedom movements to slur, to slump, to a damnable vacancy.[22] The two patrolmen who beat and killed Rafael/Horacio in this way on July 30, 1971, in Camden were suspended, but they were ultimately acquitted of manslaughter, and each continued to work for the Camden Police through many more seasons and summers. Rafael/Horacio's father filed a lawsuit. According to newspaper reports, when word came that his son's death would be settled for $15,000, the father, a merchant marine, was away at sea. The settlement offer arrived some five years after his son's death.[23]

In the narrative of Camden's political histories, of this uprising as riot and economic ruination, the son's death figures centrally. Just $5,000 of the monetary settlement came from the city; the rest, from its insurance agency, the Insurance Company of North America.[24] Rafael/Horacio was kept alive on life support, made to live, in the days between July 31, August 21, and September 15, in order to stall what was imagined as a potential escalation of violence. That the insurance settlement would be used to cover hospital bills is staggering in this sense. That his body appears and is tethered to Camden's imagined breach and indebted to what thereafter is figured as the city's perpetual loss or recovery seems incommensurable.

A spider cast a line below the porch railing. Gray bundles are holding the shape and pattern of her eggs. I trip down the steps. I grip the railing and poke her deposits, the silk sac tucked just below. It sticks to my fingers. There is a summer wind in the trees today. There is wind in the house. It comes in through the open windows. When the house is lost to us, broken, opened, vacant, or burned, it comes in everywhere and moves between treetops, and streets, and our empty rooms. The spider's lines will move this way, too, on the wind.

The slope of the floor, the angle of the wall, a busted bedroom window plugged up with a white crew sock. One of dad's lost socks! Watching the fire, keeping time with it. The climb, lick, frenzy, crack, and explosions. This bedroom had been my father's mother's, my abuelita's, too. She'd given us her house. She'd strung a line of small cast-iron bells from one of the two bedroom windows. Left them when she moved away. The bells would sound if someone who'd climbed up the porch rails and made their way onto the roof tried to get in through the window, to come into the house sideways. I take down the bells, untie all the knots, and replace the string. They are hanging at my window now, a different window in another house, next to a soft pouch on a string where I stashed a bit of my daughter's umbilical cord. I don't know why these bits of skin, cloth, and metal matter, but they hang and stake out the window.

The wood holds the burn. A summer at the steps, between a wooden porch, glass windows, metal bars and rails. No indentations there; everything is so light. Maybe you are looking out the busted window, and you finally get what you like about this city. All the kids are walking home and playing their way outside. The shape of the houses, the mix and turn of lots and vacants. Maybe this looks ugly to a lot of people. Maybe it is ugly. But you start to feel a lot of love for what you are seeing, and a general sense of peace. Memory is strung together like this, at kinship with a landscape and a people, the exhaust of a corner or a day.

ONE

Toward Camden

I want to work it this way, in coded memory,
as the history of no repair, as the ongoing
event of more and less than representing.
—FRED MOTEN, "B 4"

I lose my grounding in spring. Mornings I open my eyes and thoughts and sounds come racing. I can't sleep or rest. A few friends gather and gift me a one-way plane ticket that will get me as close to Camden as Baltimore. They see me off at the airport. I travel home at ninety-eight pounds. I break down quietly in the sky. It goes unnoticed, except by a young man who is seated next to me. Another Latino in the middle seat. He sees my head on the tray table. He asks me if I am ok. He presses his call button to get me some pain medication from the flight attendant when I lie and tell him that I just have a headache. The flight attendant brings me some aspirin from her personal stash. My parents pick me up from the airport. From there we make the few hours' drive home, toward Camden. Every now and then, to help keep him awake, my mother rubs the back of my father's neck. My father has not taken his medications so that he can drive tonight.

In a Connecticut hospital delivery room, the doctor turns away from my mother after I am born to address my father:

Would you like me to tie her tubes?
    My mother says that my father went through the roof.
    What did Dad say?
    He went through the roof!

In the year I am born, Puerto Rican women are being sterilized in hospitals left and right. My mother was born in a house in Barranquitas, Puerto Rico. A midwife delivered her, and a midwife delivered her mother too. My grandmother, my mother's mother, was sterilized in a hospital during the height of the sterilization campaigns in Puerto Rico. I do not think my grandmother ever recovered from that, and I'll make it present in the delivery room now (and finger it back into the first few pages of the prologue, too), when the doctor turns to my father in the newness of my life to ask his permission to sterilize my mother, and he, my father, goes off.

My little sister is home now, too, in Camden. She has left Parsons, where she was studying illustration, and is living upstairs in our childhood bedroom with her baby, a daughter, my niece. Tonight, my sister has written her nickname for me on a small white envelope. She tapes her gift to the television set in the living room, so that I'll see it first thing when I arrive. Inside the envelope she has placed a necklace. Mary dangles from the end of thin gold. She's figured as a saint in her robes. That night and for the next year I will sleep downstairs on a twin bed set up next to the clothes dryer in the small dining room. Between the warmth of the dryer humming and tossing wet clothes at my feet, and the view of my parents eating their lunches at the dining room table, I come back.

The school nurse makes me call home. It is late morning. As always, only my father is home. The car is broken down, so he arrives at my middle school, Veterans Memorial, on foot to pick me up. He is in the loose comfort of his house clothes. A boxy old copper sweater, navy pants that hit the ankle. He is sockless in black dress shoes. Your outfits follow the same arrangement. He has recently shaved his beard, and this makes his face appear fatter. He is thirty-nine years old. Between his fatness and the fade of poverty he looks altogether soft, except for his eyes, which shine radiant and sharp, seeing somewhere else probably too. Has it always been this way for my father?

My father hasn't had a job for many years. Once he was a counselor at Step Up, an organization in North Camden for people living with narcotics dependency (some thread of what killed his own father), and then he left that job and reenlisted in the military, this time to join the Navy (some years after a tour as a Marine in Vietnam). My father says he enlisted in the Marines strategically. He says he needed to get the kind of training that he thought would keep him alive. Given that the draft was in effect, this seemed like a choice. In 1980 my father got sick on a US Navy ship in the middle of the sea. The weight of the other war was still on him, along with all the other things he carried, and he was sent home. I remember when he came home, the joy. A knock on the door at nighttime, he wanted to surprise us:

Open the door. It's your father!

In 1987 when I am sick in middle school my father and I walk the few blocks home together. We walk down North 27th Street. So far it is the only time that the two of us have walked the Camden city streets together. Dad is into cars. He prefers to drive. It turns out I was not sick. I was just hungry. My father is kind about all of this.

When my father goes upstairs during the daytime to quiet his mind, to retreat, he tells my mother it is to rock:

Honey, I'm going upstairs to rock for a while.

And if you stand in the small narrow hallway that separates two bedrooms, you will see him there, lying down in the bed with a pillow over his head, rocking himself and a few stowaway cats to sleep.

One night a bat flies around the darkness of my parent's bedroom. I stand in the doorway, awestruck and still. I suppose he could have just opened the window and waited for it to fly out, but instead my father uses his sabana, a faded pink cotton bed sheet that is so old it has become sheer, to net and free the bat himself.

It is the usual stuff that sets the house on edge: my father misplaces his eyeglasses or loses his car keys again or upsets my mother because he's set a good cooking pot outside on the curb to catch the oil he's draining from his car.

In 2010, Dad's hoarse in a fresh robe and slippers. It is unlike him to wear a robe during the daytime or to remove his shoes or to wear slippers. He's standing sideways in a hallway on a pay phone in the Philadelphia

Veterans Affairs hospital. He has checked in against his own wishes. He tells me not to be fooled. He says: This (the VA) is not a hospital. This is a prison. He says this mostly in Spanish, to try to outwit or carve away some privacy here, away from the folks who are working or the other patients who are standing around him and who are also waiting to use the pay phone.

Esto no es un hospital, my dear. Esto es una prisión.

It is a long drive to the Coatesville Veterans Affairs hospital in 1986. Sunlight breaks at my window, all the colors of fall are in the trees and a blessed sleep arrives for the sisters, four girls in the back seat of their uncle's car. Our father is unbuckled upfront, turning this way and that way, wedged between Mom and his oldest brother, our Tío C, who is at the wheel. Dad is so intelligent and so sharp and so funny. It cuts at their talk of commitment.

Massive destruction occurred in Vietnam. Dad's disfigured by war. Agent Orange and tumors cut away: first a whole testicle and then some thirty years later a baseball-size tumor in the jaw. Anchora, Coatesville, the Philly VA. A lot of pills; not too many doctors, a few.

At the VA bus stop in Philadelphia several men board the bus. The softness of aging brown and black faces. Maybe everybody boarding the bus has a similar wide-eyed look, because it is very slippery? The snow is melting outside, and the bus does not wait for you to sit down before it takes off. Some of the men have walkers, too, which they will collapse once seated. Gravel and pitch, a slight slur. Maybe it is a medication side effect? I don't know. But in their voices, a sound like my dad's sound. There is camaraderie in a greeting. In the front of the bus, a greeting called between two African American men sanctifies the front of the bus:

Hello, my beloved.

Like my father they are remembering, injured, seeking, and aging together.

A general feeling of warmth. It greets me. It happens again and again here. On and off the bus, daily routines. Off the bus nod. The men are slightly stooped, leaning on canes, but forward-going and sure-footed once they disembark. A beauty and a history there, in the walk. After one of my sisters tells me she watched a Facebook Live video of our cousin who runs to her father and embraces him, after Hurricane Maria, after her father has made it out, off the island, I get it. That we cannot run and embrace our father. It isn't because our legs don't run. We have never really had that. We don't know that. So, we reach out in language, and perhaps we do it alone. Wonder what it is like to get to do that? Run and greet your father with a hug. Beside it all, I am grateful for the opening of a public bus, where we can sit and imagine and get a sense of each other's struggles, that vibe sometimes. Say home gone. Say not father. But turning it all over again, searching it, making it. Feeling close to it all then.

In 1985 Dad pulls a dining room chair into the living room so that he can reach the top of the door. He uses a dark blue marker to print at the arch:
Yahweh Elohim Sebaot
Perched at this angle he's got a shaky hand. From the couch we contemplate his block letters, wonder what it all means and what it will all mean in this position, hanging over our heads and our coming and going. Dad's words adorn our doorway for many years until my oldest sister decides to paint the room. She climbs the same chair and drags a handheld brush across the last physical traces of our father's message. Maybe she only applies one coat or maybe it's just cheap paint, because eventually the submerged letters show through, a harmony of my sister and my father at the woodwork.

In 1985 he converts the living room into his study and exiles my sisters and me upstairs. That's how we take it. We curse him silently and often. Upstairs is an oven in the summer. We mourn the loss of the only air conditioner and the television set. He's gotten his GED and now he's trying to use the GI Bill to get his BA. He's blazing at a million watts. He's enrolled at Rutgers University in Camden, but the GE required math is kicking his ass. They make him take it first; it is a prerequisite. It's too bad. He soars through cultural anthropology, but under the stress of math he eventually gives out and is hospitalized. He never returns to school after that.

While Dad is in Coatesville our house is broken into for the first time. As we pull up in our uncle's Blazer I watch what looks like a young white woman with blonde hair spot our approach and hurry away. She's the lookout so she moves pretty fast, but never runs. All they take is our television set. The knobs were broken off, and we had to use a pair of pliers to change the channels, but still. We cry. It is all very stressful, but one day we are able to make jokes about it. Our uncle, my father's eldest brother, uses a collection of two-by-fours to nail shut the back door off the kitchen. The robbers had kicked that door in to access the house and all of our stuff. When Dad gets out of Coatesville hospital he buys us a brand new TV that comes with a remote control. The back door stays boarded up for some years more until a man from our church, newly arrived from Puerto Rico (he has that warmth), prods it open from the inside. He fixes it for us and then the backyard air and the sunshine pour in.

Many years before, when we lived at East State Street Village, a low-rise project in East Camden (the kind I got to see pictured in HBO's *The Wire*), my father woke up my older sisters and made them go pick berries with him. The night before, they had assembled their uniforms: long-sleeved shirts and bandanas to protect their faces and hair. They rode a bus with many other Latino people, traveling to a farm somewhere in South Jersey to pick the berries or whatever was being harvested. My sisters left with him before first light and came home that night, exhausted. They were twelve or thirteen years old at the time. My little sister and I were too young to go, so we never got to see the shape of them, our big sisters working outdoors, but I remember the looks on their faces when they arrived home. My father was trying to make and save money to pay tuition, so he could go to seminary school. What binds my parents is some part of our twinned inheritance—an all-abiding and desperate love of God and study.

They met inside a Pentecostal church in Bridgeport, Connecticut, in 1965. My mother was seated with her three sisters in a circle of folding chairs. They were in skirts and studying and talking *La Biblia*. My father recognizes the face of a gentle God, but he is just seventeen so instead he tells her that she has the knees of a camel. Afterward, when they are in love and then throughout their marriage, he'll call her princess and honey and she'll call him honey and Freddy.

Something he reads in a book he checks out of the public library, a picture of Catholic benevolence. A little boy, Dad walks to the convent in Bridgeport and shows the nuns his broken shoes. They ask him where he lives and later they come knocking on his door, with a box of food and things for the children. His family is thankless—he has betrayed their poverty—but soon they all turn to God.

He is with his unit. They are washing in a river when a mortar hits. It is February 1968, the Tet Offensive. He is naked, running away from the waters when he buckles. He is dragged away. The medic shakes his head. It is a small wound at the knee. He'll be patched up easy, sent to China Beach to recover. Dad says most everyone was wiped out. He says he didn't graduate from high school or college, so this is as close as he'll get to reunion, this memory of the last time they were together, as young men, but still, he does not want to remember.

My little sister used to bring our father his medications with a glass of orange juice so he wouldn't puke his guts out first thing in the morning. The names of these drugs sound out distant planets: haloperidol, quetiapine, lorazepam . . . He balances himself on the edge of the bed. His thinning hair stands up here and there, before he pushes it all back with one hand, and eases himself up. One leg atrophies. Pieces of shrapnel lodged forty-plus years below the knee will do that, eat away at the muscle.

Helicopters whirl, fly, drop, and fall. Years later the sounds of a propeller, a showerhead, what might rain down, will spread weeks between his baths. My father is in this condition, stalled out somewhere between memory, study, and salvation, when he picks me up from Veterans Memorial Middle School in Camden one afternoon when my hunger is mistaken for sickness.

Can you find your father? He's outside now. He's at the curb. He's rigging a ladder to the top of his pickup truck with some cord. It is hanging way too far over the front and back. He runs around in that truck. He won't get hired to fix anything and he himself is looking so particularly rundown. He's dressed up softly underneath though. He says there are cool sands and I believe he is the water.

In this one it is winter, marked February 1968. Mom is beauty standing on a New York rooftop gazing at the city below. She is a bare profile, warm in a faded brown hand-me-down coat. She says she is thinking about Dad, who has gone to war. Her lips are parted when someone snaps her picture. This letter is from my father, written by him on his twentieth birthday. This is the sound of him, his ideas, a dialogue, what she might have held midbreath:

January 22, 1968

Mi Amor,

Es mi anhelo que cuando esta carta llegue a tus manos estés gozando de las bendiciones de nuestro buen padre celestial. Y que has tenido triunfo en tu vida diaria. Amor mio, ¿cómo estás? Lleno del espíritu amén, contenta amén. Down? Ok, ok.

Well, I hope you are well darling. I love you so much. Did I ever tell you that? Querida, ¿has oído de Tony? ¿Cómo está? Y tu Mama? Escríbala y cuentale de cómo Dios me está bendiciendo pues yo la quiero mucho, aunque ella quisiera alguien de mayor edad para ti, pero que se puede hacer cuando algo, como algo de amor se trata, verdad? Querida, pronto voy a mandarte unos retratos, ok? Bueno, espero que pronto amor. Me robaron la cartera y se me han perdido todos los retratos e ID y algunos papeles! Bueno, no llevaron ningún dinero mío, pues no tengo ninguno. Y prefería perder todo el dinero que a los retratos tuyos, verdad? Bueno. ¿Tienes los negativos verdad? Hang onto them, ok?

Darling, have you ever read "The Cross and the Switchblade" or "Twelve Angels from Hell"? Well, I have and believe me I was really blessed by the Holy Ghost. I really enjoyed the experience of those addicts who became converted and cried every time one of them came trembling to God: "What a friend we have in Jesus." Amen. Darling, sometimes when I get lonely and I think of you, well especially and at night, I feel your breath on my cheeks and see your face one inch from mine. I see your face almost radiating in front of mine and there is "something" of you with me. And this "algo de ti" me acompaña cuando duermo. Que bueno, verdad? Mmmmm.

Honey, let's place a petition before the Lord. Let's ask him to do something, especially during this year for us. Do you believe in miracles? Well, I do. And I know that if we ask him he will answer, verdad? Ok. Querida, yo quiero tanto que tu te mantengas en la gracia de nuestro Señor. El puede hacer tanto para nosotros, verdad, después que ponemos todo en tus manos. Y, yo se que tu quieres servirle y amarle de todo tu alma y mente. Yo tambien lo quiero querer y amar de ese modo. Honey, me mencionas de diezmo en tu carta. Y te digo que yo no me enojo porque me lo dice. Pues, para mi se me hace mas dificil diezmar no por dinero, pero porque estoy tan lejos y ya tu vez como robaron la carta que te mande a ti. El Filipino era el souvenir, y yo aprendí por eso no mandar ningún dinero por el correo y money orders are a little hard to get on ship, I think, so don't worry, the Lord knows my heart. And I hope the pastor isn't mentioning it to you too much, because I wouldn't like to think that. He knows I haven't forgotten the church, but the church has forgotten me. Not in prayers, but a letter, even one letter of encouragement. Is this too much? You better not say nothing though, amor, people wouldn't understand. I love our church and the people in it though, but I guess it's hard for them to send one a line, and I would answer, but maybe they think I wouldn't? Well, que se puede hacer? I am not using this as an excuse, but I remember this and thought while we were "talking" about the church I would mention it.

How's Ruthie doing and Carlos? God bless them. I hope they are happy, and I know Rachel is. Is Carlos still attending church? I hope so. Tell him I said hi and that I am glad to hear he is engaged. Darling, you should see the diamond I can get hold of for an inexpensive price! Well, I can't think about that, I have to save!

So, you're planning Puerto Rico? Well, honey, I sure would like to go with you. Well, if you go have fun and do everything to his glory, verdad? And if you don't, maybe we'll go together for my first time anyway! Bueno querida, I really hope you are well, and I miss you so bad, but I don't think of it. I just think about the Lord and maybe he'll come this year and then we can be united with him in heaven, with Jesus, amen.

Each for each other, and both for the Lord. Him! Just for him, praise his name!

Well, I sign off for now. Till tomorrow, my love. Sleep well, querida! Hilda . . . Yo . . . te . . . quiero . . . wonder!

con amor de tu novio, Freddy

P.S. I still haven't heard about promotions yet. I'm on the list so I hope I get it! Good—will be brave!

It's all moving. This effort at a dialogue with his girlfriend about what it means to be churchgoing in a time of war, what it means to be of service, to tithe, and in all the fragility and tenderness of poverty, of love and belief, worth repeating, verdad? My father, who had yet to visit his ancestral Puerto Rico, a Puerto Rican in Vietnam. Mom says that in the months after he is wounded he flings it all away. He breaks up with her. Most everyone is dead in his platoon. He is in the pits. It seems these bits are the last of Dad, before some of the horror that would seep in and never let go. I've asked Mom whether she can pick a letter from Dad for this project or send me what she's got. She kindly agrees.[1] She used to keep the letters in her bedroom closet in Camden. She kept them in a black plastic garbage bag. As a girl, I'd read them in my searches through all my mother's things. Sounding out the Spanish words, skipping over what I didn't understand. Holding their privacy inside my own. When I ask her to look for the letters she says she cannot find them. She says she fears they are in the basement, in Camden. That they were moved there and that when the house was broken into and the copper pipes were stolen and the basement flooded, the letters were destroyed. I don't think this is the case, that the letters decomposed in Camden, in the watery basement mix of all our precious and packed-away stuff. But I marvel at the turn of fate, where the one letter she could find would be a letter Dad wrote on his birthday, a letter in which he makes no mention that it is his birthday, but instead plays at the bottom of the page with the future, with their marriage, the transformation of Mom's name to his name. Dad would be wounded a few weeks later, in February the unkind.

In 2001, six months after I've returned home, my friend who has a dissertation fellowship in Carlisle, Pennsylvania, drives a rental car to our house in Camden for a Thanksgiving visit. I double up with my big sister on the sofa bed in the living room so he can have my bed in the dining room. He'll sleep just a couple of feet from the table, but I don't think anything of it. I figure a built-in trust, because he gifted me a one-way ticket home, because he's Chicano and he grew up working poor, too, but in Whittier, California, and I trust he gets it, the everyday arrangements of tight living that make life in common possible and aren't only reserved for the holidays.

When I agree, my mother sets up a time for me to go see Dr. Brenner. A family practitioner in Camden, Dr. Brenner is my mother and sister's doctor, and he recently delivered my niece. My sister tells me he encouraged her all the way, for a natural delivery. The kind of "you can do it" practiced by a mentor. He is kind to my family, and I trust that. From our house it is a good walk to Dr. Brenner's office, just down River Road. He tells my mother that I am very sick. I can't recall whether I am in the room when he tells her that. If not, he tells mom and she tells me. All the boundaries are porous. I am gifted a small white bag, the kind we used to stuff with penny candies after another day of middle school and feast on while we made the short walk home, Now and Laters, Red Hots, loose wrapped bubble gum. This one is fat with free samples of just two drugs, Zyprexa and Zoloft. Once I am home, standing at the dining room table in my makeshift bedroom, I wrestle with myself about it, and then, as if

I am giving up, I take the pills. I scratch away in my journal, trace my old lines, the echoes of so many voices.

In 2001, I read *The Courier Post* want ads and I find work as a receptionist for the academic year at Camden Academy, a new charter high school. At 7:15 each weekday morning Dad wakes up and downs a cup of black coffee so that he, too, can beat his medication fog and drive me just up the way. At 3:00 in the afternoon he is outside waiting for me in his little blue Toyota Tercel, or sometimes I just walk home.

I tack up an old print on a bulletin board just behind my desk, "The Frame," one of Frida Kahlo's colorful self-portraits. Its border is shaped by flowers, a riotous assembly of red, pink, orange, and yellow buds. Two blue crested birds flank her at each shoulder. Kahlo painted this arrangement on the backside of a piece of glass and then laid it over her self-portrait, so that the frame hovers just above a saturated blue backdrop and the image of her own face, which she painted on aluminum. What I hang on the wall bears just a likeness to the mixed-media portrait: a small paper print that is worn and creased where it has been folded too many times. It tells nothing of the original's setting or construction, but it stands out against the white walls of the office and it is enough of a reminder to me of beauty in life and artistry. The students who volunteer to bring in the morning attendance report or who get sent from class to the office for disciplinary stuff consider Kahlo's uses of color and odd beauty while they wait to see the vice principal or school counselor, and sometimes they ask me about it:

Who's that? Why does she look like that?

A fellow Puerto Rican, a student named J peeks into the office often to say hello to me, and one day he sits down in one of the chairs across from the reception desk where I sit and route telephone calls, mostly from parents. I'm shy, nervous, and phone averse so I try to come up with a greeting that is welcoming, short, and graceful, and then I memorize it. This feels like an accomplishment:

Good morning [or good afternoon], Camden Academy High School. This is Mercy speaking. How can I help you?

It is just the two of us in the office, as the administrators are out and about, and so I ask him:

What's going on?

He tells me that his Spanish teacher (who will end up leaving the school at the end of the year to pursue another degree, an MBA) has said (within earshot of all his classmates) that the boy's family are probably drug dealers. J is offended and so he goes off. The teacher kicks him out of the classroom and sends him to the office. I offer to help him to complete some of his other work while he cools out and waits for one of the administrators to return. He's got to write a haiku as an assignment for another class. We sit and imagine together. What's a slow-motion scene, but something that is also in the quick of it? He says when his sister comes out onto the porch to call him inside. We try to work out the scene in the syllables. We consider the beauty of it all: of his older sister and his evening turn away from the street and up the porch, arroz con pollo for dinner inside, the changing colors of a Camden sky, and you are most certainly loved. We want to make something that gathers from his every day. We know what's going on there with that teacher, but we don't talk about it. We focus on the poem instead.

J is best school friends with Berto, another African American and Puerto Rican boy. Berto wears his hair out, a long and loose Afro that makes him stand taller than his peers and a few of the teachers too. He seems to get into a lot of trouble, and he likes to laugh. I gift him a copy of Abraham Rodriguez's novel *The Buddha Book*. I think he will like it, the story of high schoolers who compose a comic book series together. Everything that they represent in their comic book has to be true. It has to have already happened. When they get mixed up with a murder they find themselves having to represent it, bound by their own ethics and genre. I'm right. Berto really gets into the book. From my desk I see him walking the hallway reading it, trailing a bunch of other kids. He towers and the sight of him read-walking fills me with some kind of joy. The history teacher, who is also African American and who I come to consider a friend, stops in often to pick up his office mail and we'll chat. After he reads a bit of my writing, the bits I compose into my workday when there isn't too much going on, he tells me that when he reads he imagines the characters as himself and his wife. I don't do that as a reader, and I wonder about it. What looseness of character allows the reader to flow in? Or what tight familiar? He is all a-wonder at Berto, who is his student and who apparently doesn't seem to have done a lick of schoolwork up until this point. And this *The Buddha Book* reading won't count for a grade. A few days later Berto is bookless. I wonder if he's already finished. He tells me it was stolen. This book stealing stuns and amazes me.

Berto, where's the book?

Somebody stole it.

A few months later Berto is expelled from the school, for fighting off campus. I am upset by it all, by the punishment. Especially because it happened offsite, so I think maybe it shouldn't count as much. But the history teacher tells me it wasn't a fair fight, that Berto jumped some other kid, and that he beat that kid up pretty badly. Maybe somebody can jump Berto and reset the balance? Maybe he can be forgiven? I think a lot of things, just in the interest of keeping the boy here with us in school and watching him grow up more. Before he goes, Berto comes into the office and gifts me a small pin. It is an American flag, the kind politicians wear on their lapels to denote their patriotism, that they are not traitors, but the pin has lost its catch so it cannot be secured. I wonder whether he knows that Abraham Rodriguez has another book, a collection of stories called *The Boy without a Flag*, but I do not get to ask him. I'll ask him here.

Rasheeda comes into the office regularly. Like J and Berto, she's a ninth grader. They are the first class, and as they grow the school will continue to add grades and add students. So, it is a small school and Rasheeda seems to be friends with most everyone. Sometimes bringing in the attendance report, sometimes when she is sent out of class, sometimes when she just wants to say hello and chat between classes. All the students call me Miss Mercy no matter how much I tell them they can drop the *Miss* and just call me by my name. For me this play is some part of the love and respect of being called home. Rasheeda is about fourteen years old that year, tall and lanky. I see her in the mornings and at the end of each day, too, and by then her hair usually strays from her ponytail and her uniform's a bit untucked. Like Berto, she has a really good sense of humor and we are able to laugh together. Little sounds escape, as if her voice wants to sing out. She'll say something and then something else will emerge, another sound. Everyone calls her Piggy. When I am gone, well enough to get back to graduate school in California, Rasheeda reaches out to me via email, to invite me to join her network on Blackplanet.com. These kids pose with me at the end of the year in goodbye pictures. They know I am leaving again. Looking at those pictures today, I'm awed that my own son is about the age they were then. This child is precious to me. I see him. And reckoning with their gifts, their tenderness, at school, toward me, it leaves me so full and it flowers, even still.

In December 2012, I learn that Rasheeda has died. That she has been killed in Camden. The grassroots organization STOP (Stop Trauma on People) erects a cross for her on the lawn outside of City Hall. Cross #67 is designated with her name. She is shot as she answers her door, and she passes in the parking lot just outside her apartment. From online reading I learn that her neighbors say she is self-sufficient and good; she had her own place. The media points out that she has no "record," and all wonder how can this be? In 2015 I look for pictures, because even after almost three years of knowing, I still cannot believe that this has happened to her. It does not make sense to me. It won't settle down as something that has happened or that I know. I wonder, can it really be true? But when I see her picture, lay it over her name, it is, it is her. It takes me years to do this. She has the same lovely face, fuller at age twenty-five. She is designated murder "#67" in Camden in 2012. When I am writing this, it is only after I have gotten up multiple times and walked around the room. The reading is the same. Look up and out. You might get up and try to work it out, so that you can grieve. I read that Rasheeda made music. I hear Rasheeda recorded her raps. I search out a recording online and yes, her friend who is grieving, too, has posted a track, and he gifts us all. I get to hear her voice, and she is representing for Camden a lot in each of her verses. I recognize the sound of her voice, the edges and the richness of what she sounded like at fourteen. I read in a newspaper article that Rasheeda struggled to overcome Tourette syndrome. To use her voice as an expressive vehicle, to achieve lyric and song. The control of it all, the technicality of what it means to spit, the rhyme and condensed poetry of rap. Her struggle and talents crystallize and fold.

Bit by bit thoughts join course. But you are never the same. You are on the other side now, full of compassion.

Why should I write like that here? It won't come that other way to me anyway, and this represents a kind of failure, but I am okay with that. In 2001 I came home and found myself in a circle, the trusted community of Camden students, of mother, father, sisters, and nieces, of new friends and a practicing doctor in this place. These stories are those that turn there, here, together, that accompany me in Camden (when I loved, and I was gifted love and loved back to life).

In 2014 Dr. Brenner was recognized for his work in Camden with a MacArthur Fellowship. The story of how he mapped patient needs, particularly in the high-rise Northgate II apartments, changed the narrative and understanding of a landscape of care for the residents of that place.

A 2011 *New Yorker* article entitled "The Hot Spotters," written by Atul Gawande, profiles Dr. Brenner and his practice, the "cheaply constructed, boxlike, one-story building on a desolate street of bars, car repair shops, and empty lots."[2] But we can reset the scene, maybe work some against extraction and accounting. The people come and go, also in all their lively complexities, histories, and along beloved grounds. Lives made visible by everyday acts and made invisible by structures of violence and the public languages and easy discourses of criminality that threaten to seize us all. You might walk to the doctor's office and this is not what you see or feel. You remember otherwise, you feel otherwise. New music is in you; there is song. This carries you through every doorway and along the fences and your vision passes along who is working at the repair shop and if or when you are better or older maybe things will be different, and you can meet someone and go for an after-work drink at one of those bars. This neighborhood is yours. And so, love scrapes by, and that, too, is perhaps a kind of common desolation.

Dr. Brenner's family practice site on River Road closed in 2009. Gawande's *New Yorker* piece tells the story of how, after sitting on a police oversight commission and reflecting on a growing number of murders in Camden, Dr. Brenner began tinkering with information to create a data set that he then plotted onto a map. These experiences, what had happened there, he believed, might inform and generate another kind of policing. A concentrated preventive presence that might act as a deterrent to violent crime and secure the neighborhood for its residents. The presence of patrolling police, say, on foot or in a car, may cause enough of a visual disruption, signaling that the landscape was no longer open or available for certain kinds of activities. Within this framework the block's radius would become more livable for the people residing there. So that they wouldn't have to be afraid to come outside and be subject to or witness new violence or new death. Suspended from his mapping project (and Gawande's narrative) was the idea that policing itself generates fear and violence. The doctor's map work, however, was understood as a kind of arrogance and an overstepping of boundaries and was unwelcomed by the police force at the time. They were not interested in the doctor's numbers and what the numbers claimed to lay bare, historical, and/or predictable.

Dr. Brenner, however, had uncovered a usable and duplicatable method of mapping, where numbers could register, expose, and disperse complex experiences and chart a set of coordinates that might lead somewhere else. Rejected, he then translated this method to his own field, to health care and emergency department visits. Dr. Brenner gathered economic figures and mapped them as coordinates to uncover the figure of a residential tower. Northgate II tower is a high rise at the edge of the water and the foot of the Benjamin Franklin Bridge. The people with the most chronic needs, as betrayed by his map, were found to be living together there. Their need was described via the economic assembly and criminality of the "hot spot," the microgeographic language of place-based policing that exploits the gathering site toward disruption, displacement, and capture. The hot spot is the language of biosurveillance, of concentrated policing and the management of care. Indeed, Dr. Brenner's interest in this method seems to have emerged from his introduction to the popularized (and debunked) "broken windows theory" and his interest in former New York City Police Commissioner William Bratton's computerized crime maps, known as the Compstat approach to community policing. At the heart of this theory of comfort in a normative visual order is a form of policing that disrupts a publicly criminalized aesthetic to provide a conduit for desirable movement and people along a landscape. Violent crime is absented via misdemeanor policing, the arrangement of a generalized and pleasing controlled material landscape.[3] The appropriate looks of a landscape do not end at the window, but seep into appropriate bodies in place and in motion, stop-and-frisk campaigns, gang injunctions, the snapshot precrime logic of racial profiling that hinges upon a racialized aesthetic and antiblackness.

Dr. Brenner's data attempted to illuminate another set of practices for reducing costs and reinscribed a debt model of health toward a practice of care.[4] His numbers, the lives and experiences represented in those numbers, were not evacuated of their specificity but were brought under the map light in order to secure a fact, the precision of expenditure. The box in here would allow each person to choose services in place in life. That is to say, a doctor may come to you. Pain management and the long haul of getting better at home. A clinician and then a social worker. We can try to shake loose the fear of the coupling. The grossness of symptoms pulled away from a life or a life extracted to sociological study. You can be in community, because relations of care will build you up. So that you do not find yourself wheeled out in a crisis and set upon by the fluorescent lights of the emergency department and the sirens of an ambulance or squad car. Can a mapping project enable you to stay put? Can a social worker leave you alone or stay out of your "business," as one Northgate II resident wondered and worried?

What does it mean that we must make ourselves all around known? Hurry up off the page as legible data, a population, a people relegated to a (chosen) place too? That is one axis, one boundary, of care. It has its dangers. Embedded at the origin, a notion of a more benevolent policing and the mythological pinpoint accuracy of data. Technologies of care that may rehabilitate a therapeutic and disciplinary state and its appeal to recognition, to getting well or being good. At the map coordinates Camden is an unplace, a nonplace, bereft of histories of colonialism and white supremacy. To disidentify in place, with your body, with your historical present, yet to gear up for the future, a team-driven wellness practice that infiltrates your place with social workers, health care workers, and a clinic. A possible you, a possible body, when your home place is opened up to the state in Camden. This opening is not a metaphor. In 2008 helicopters landed on the roof of Northgate I tower, and militarized police dropped from above to secure the floor of the building known as "Little Iraq."[5]

The Northgate towers are a pair of high rises in a place of low rises. The landscape here in places comprises empty lots that spread and no longer hold their shape. A single building stands, where all the others have been torn down or are falling apart. Accustomed as we were to the low rises, and never having entered the Northgate Towers, they had a Jeffersons' feel for me growing up, as any high rise did: a bit of glamour, fantasy, and possibility in the elevatored building that reaches for the sky. They were designed with this call in mind. A set of luxury towers to bring forth monied residents to hold this stretch of Camden.

The Northgate II Tower was completed in 1962 and has twenty-one floors. Like Northgate I, it offers vistas. From the Northgate Towers you can see the waters of the Delaware River. The vision might transcend the noise. The open-landscape vacants that compose the landscape might also transcend the noise. A quiet exists in these arrangements and in this place (for me). It is a part of my life. You can run through it or you can get run down. You can be run down here. I was. I can be here, and I can be abundant, and I can be run down, which is what I feel sometimes and a lot of what I am, even in the best of times. There is a quality of vitality in letting loose on what is real. That people are open to it all. We take it all in. We suffer it. This can be the grounds.

Photographer Camilo José Vergara maps out his philosophies, at one point following J. B. Jackson, about what they call the "necessity of ruins." What kinds of self-making practices can emerge in this place where you are in touch with the ruin? Where it is visible from on high. Felt below. When "in touch" means you walk it, you gotta walk on by and through. Maybe you will never get or have the kind of mindset that says rebuild toward another aesthetic. Some of Vergara's photographic panoramas of North Camden are captured from inside Northgate I tower. Channel these sounds, colors, textures. See the world. See a bit of green. See a brown freckled lot after a light snow.

The information that Dr. Brenner collected and assembled as data and as debt said that residents here were using the emergency department as a site of primary care. It was expensive and alarming. Collectively, the tower residents' visits to the emergency department were a drain and a drag on a system of taxpayer payment and expense.

What kind of pain forces you up and out at night? What chronic pains get you to the ER? The run and get to the hospital, crisis of body and the things you fare and go through there. The rush and haste, all the people. The wait and the unwelcome. They were everyday and ordinary American illnesses, diabetes mostly.

Camden has emerged as a model site for rethinking disease and care. Not the violence of poverty itself, but a method and an extracted set of practices that could tell about a larger model of care for a more general population. Camden community policing has also emerged as a model of policing. The histories of surveillance as safety in Camden. How are these informational systems different from the eye-in-the-sky cameras being used to watch the streets? In each is a kind of timeline of violence—the potential in both scenes to effect change—yet the live camera sees, and the mapping sees after, collects and archives information to predict and intercede in a predictable future.

Camden Coalition of Healthcare Providers, the organization that grew out of Dr. Brenner's research, focuses on clients and patients who are "ready for change." The focus here—the understanding of an agency or a desire in being ready—denotes a relationship to time and a break or turning point toward another kind of future, another kind of health and body. If you are not ready you might hold and waste time, resources; but, too, it is good to know where you are and decide to stay that way, stay it in. You are always in it anyway? My father is a chronic emergency department user. He's a drag and a drain and a debt. But it is not him; it is what happened to him. And it cannot be undone, a war. That he is in it, in that meaning, strikes me as ethical.

TWO

Empty
Lots

Thou foster-child of silence and slow time.
—JOHN KEATS, "Ode on a Grecian Urn"

Before it was destroyed by fire, the corner lot at North 27th Street and Lincoln Avenue held an abandoned duplex. Many of the neighborhood's boys spent afternoons and evenings there before the fire, sitting high on that stoop. We lived across the street. The 1991 "Mischief Night" fire that destroyed that house burned quietly at first. In our house my father slept, my mother did the bills, and I finished up my homework, a paper on a poem about a beautifully etched vase. The fire outside cast an orange glow to our upstairs, melting the siding of our house. We were made to evacuate in case it should spread. We watched from outside now, as the fire was put out, and what was once a crack house, more or less structurally in shape, became another kind of ruin. The burnt remains would sit for some more years, mostly as an unmoored porch, until they were finally and completely demolished.

On Mischief Night of 1991, Camden, New Jersey, was swept by fire. The house on the corner was just one of a recorded forty-nine structures that burned down on the night of October 30 and into the early morning hours of Halloween, when the fire department responded to 150 alarms.[1] In an open letter addressed "to all personnel involved" with the Camden Fires, then fire chief Kenneth Penn wrote: "What occurred during Mischief Night '91 was the single busiest tour of duty in the 122 year history of the Camden Fire Department. Only the urban riots of the 1970's [sic] saw more overall fire activity over a period of several days but not in the short span of time that we incurred on the evening [of] October 30, 1991. Some 150+ alarms were serviced within a very brief period. What our Fire Control Force accomplished during that short time may never be surpassed."[2]

Though characterized as random acts of arson throughout the city (vacant buildings and brush as the remains of the previous fires, the overgrowth), we can understand the fires, when taken together, as a space-clearing gesture, an organized and purposeful message about histories, abandonment, and vulnerability—that is, the very full life of Camden's "leftover" structural forms and grounds.[3] The following year, a curfew was imposed in Camden; it was directed at African American and Latinx youth, who were imagined as the source of the fires. In the *New York Times* article "Camden Braces for Mischief Night Fires," Reverend Michael Doyle, an Irish priest who worked in Camden for more than thirty-five years, critiqued the curfew: "I'd rather all this strength and mobilization be channeled toward the rehabilitation of housing which wouldn't leave them vulnerable to being burned."[4] In this statement Reverend Doyle, affectionately termed Camden's "poet of poverty," shifts the idea of curfew— what in Camden would delineate a further limitation of (social) movement—to offer instead a critique of structural abandonment.[5]

Understanding the segregation of Camden, New Jersey, as a hyperghetto, the everyday horizon of social violence embedded in abandoned buildings and vacant lots, and the epistemic violence inherent to ongoing discourses of revitalization and redevelopment, is an exercise in sifting through the rubble of white supremacy and political corruption. A largely African American and Latino town, Camden has made the impossible list of cities "past the point of no return" and has achieved the status of a so-called permanent ghetto.[6] Camden's organized abandonment, the racialization of poverty, arrived in the form of deindustrialization and "suburban sprawl." Camden city's population has declined by 40 percent since the 1950s. Today Camden is one of the poorest cities in the United States, with a poverty rate at 42.5 percent. The city's murder rate "has escalated to the highest of any city in the United States with more than 65,000 inhabitants."[7]

Camden is overwhelmed by structural violence and is mostly dogged at representation. Across television, print, and social media, the city has a stricken pose. It has been imagined as a "ghastly poorhouse," its landscapes represented as (racial, sexual, and economic) grotesque, and its current residents as simultaneously outside of the human and without attachment. When Camden draws comparisons, other places are lifted and unnatural catastrophes are invoked—Detroit, Beirut, Katrina, Fallujah—a severed collection of local and global forces to serve as metaphors for the catastrophic visual life of a fallen landscape. Indeed, that 1992 *New York Times* article, "Camden Braces for Mischief Night Fires," references the imaginary that dogs Camden everywhere: the racialized fall, the gendered slide, where what was upright is now unstable. Within this framework, the city in "braces," we witness a suspended collapse and wonder how to shore up the fall or have a hand in another kind of movement. From the *New York Times* article: "With nearly half of its 87,462 residents receiving some sort of public assistance, Camden is the poorest urban area in New Jersey and one of the poorest cities in the nation. Once a thriving industrial city that was home to shipyards and the Campbell Soup Company, Camden began its economic and social slide in the 1950's [*sic*] as white residents started moving to the suburbs. Between 1950 and 1980, the city lost nearly one-third of its population. Thousands of buildings were left vacant, and the closing of the shipyards and the Campbell plant hastened the slide."[8]

We arrived in Camden after the 1970 riots, the event that the Camden City fire chief drew a comparison to in 1991, those several days in 1971 when the city was on fire. We arrived just a few years later, but the matter was still present (as it is today): a landscape remade at conflict, a boarded up boulevard, what might have once been a row of stores. I grew up not knowing or asking why, but wondering about the organization of space, finding peace and meaning in this aesthetic. A collection of buildings are boarded up, and the windows protrude for display—yes, you can tell that used to be a storefront. That something had happened here, a physical reality, an extension of some catastrophe, a war. That we were living in the aftermath, had somehow missed it. And so, you might feel your way through everything daily, a girl on a walk to and from school, the gentle fade of an abandoned row. Some architecturally ornate detail now on its side or last leg, the boarded-up cover-up and all of you on the outside of these histories, but in them too.

In the opening pages of *Camden after the Fall: Decline and Renewal in a Post-Industrial City*, historian Howard Gillette recounts his attempts to trace Camden City's most recent history. He finds rotting documents and the overwhelming mismanagement of public records: "In Camden, the condition of public records, like much of the rest of the city's infrastructure, is extremely poor."[9] Gillette thus reconstructs a historical narrative, using interviews of current and former residents, activists, and public officials. Of Camden, Gillette writes: "While Camden offers a small stage, all the major issues associated with the descent of the classic blue-collar city appear *on it* in recognizable form and in comprehensible fashion."[10]

If, like the city, as surface, Camden's vacant or empty lots also offer a "small stage," then I am interested in the empty lot as an expressive ground that inspires and arranges a repertoire of (nonviolent) movements. Performance studies scholar Diana Taylor describes the repertoire as embodied knowledge/practice: "a way of thinking through movement" as well a conduit for the transmission of memory.[11] What are the forms of living, of nonviolent movement at these Camden sites? What does it mean to sit in a place overrun in structural violence, to sit high, to imagine, to pray, to stumble, run, or cut across space? The vacant lot seeps and contains, it deforms a block and curbs an experience with the sidewalk. Depending on what is happening there, a pedestrian may walk in the street to avoid a lot, or she may cut across it, bisecting the sidewalk and the distance between two points.[12] Recalling the downward imaginary of the city's slow decline, it becomes critical for us to think about modes of perhaps indiscernible movement in Camden that are made in relation to a fall, that is, at landscapes that buckle, crumble, and overgrow. How does a spatial configuration render a sense of movement, an embodiment that both performs dispossession and is site specific? As that which is lively and performed, a fall radically resists the stilled extraction and the smooth recuperation of analysis; it underscores the dimensions of a spatial existence that cannot be captured or reduced to the erasure or easy incorporation of representational projects of recovery.[13]

As they are produced in the service of surveillance, representations of life in Camden recoil as the spectacular and grotesque and, I would argue, find a performative and generative countermovement in Camden. That is, what does it mean to move and make lively degraded space?[14] What is at stake here is an ethical understanding of life in place and a re-visioning of "vacant" space that begins at, rather than recovers, a deformation. This re-visioning becomes historically relevant and urgent given the most recent history in the Cramer Hill neighborhood, the site of that vacant lot at North 27th and Lincoln Avenue, where the threat of eminent domain hinged on the racialized language of revitalization, which reduced the landscape and its forms of living to a representational message—a message about definitions of appropriate and profitable public use and play; the mapping, representation, and appropriation of spaces; and the condemnation of racialized public looks and behaviors.[15]

No Cherokee

In 2003, Cramer Hill, a largely African American and Latina neighborhood on the east side of Camden, New Jersey, became the target of a $1.2 billion privately funded neighborhood redevelopment plan.[16] The vacant lot at North 27th Street and Lincoln Avenue constituted a border of the Cherokee Redevelopment Plan in that neighborhood. Cherokee Investment Partners' plan in Camden included using eminent domain to acquire uninhabited properties and displace current residents toward achieving "smart growth" and "new urbanism movements." Although Cramer Hill's waterfront location and economic and population stability (imagined in comparison with those of other Camden neighborhoods) made it a desirable location for redevelopment, this stability also became the grounds for the dispossession of current residents. That is, the greening and creation of new and diverse neighborhoods was directed toward unsettling a Puerto Rican and African American community; within the terms of this redevelopment, their value was constituted by their ability to become figures, empty, displaced and camouflaged by a generalized ruined and open landscape.

Residents, however, mobilized their outrage at the racialized discourses of redevelopment (rehabilitation and underperformance), particularly via grassroots meetings and a visual protest movement, a leaflet and poster campaign. "No Cherokee" flyers went up, strategically and meaningfully, everywhere. The grassroots use of images, posters in the windows of homes, on telephone poles and abandoned buildings, initiated another reading: a revaluation of homes and landscapes largely relegated to the "unsightly." Given the threat of eminent domain within the terms of redevelopment, the "No Cherokee" posters in windows (which mimicked in design the iconic "No Smoking" sign) provided a critical redirection to the politics of visibility—of what constitutes private property and public use—a reinstantiation of borders between the public and (domestic) private, and an antiracist activism that threw into crisis the racialized terms of morality and the normative boundaries of race, gender, and sexuality in public space.[17]

The posters welcomed an inquiry (What is Cherokee?) while performing a refusal (No Cherokee). Like the "No Smoking" sign, the "No Cherokee" image embodied danger (of displacement) and what constitutes healthy communities and proper conduct in place.

Indeed, the Cramer Hill "No Cherokee" posters created "an imagery that evokes a place transformed by pain."[18] African Americans and Latinx people were centrally and erroneously imagined as initiating white dispossession in and flight from this neighborhood. Their presence and attachment to particular landscapes was a sign of its very underperformance.[19] Yet the fight against eminent domain mobilized their readiness to stay, and to create alternative images and forms of nonviolent movement at valuable landscapes in order to secure that future. Posters still in place (preserved behind windows, deteriorating in empty lots and on abandoned buildings) are part of a beautiful struggle, the reconstitution of solidarity and community, visuality, and the protest of poverty, and the fragmented archival landscape of collective and communal memory.

invinciblecities

In a 2006 photograph from photographer Camilo José Vergara's *invinciblecities* website, you can make out a "No Cherokee" sign on a telephone pole. Vergara creates images of "inner city" urban landscapes and has photographed Camden since 1977. *invinciblecities*, an online archive funded by the Ford Foundation, organizes Vergara's city-specific images in a database, and along an interactive map of Camden. His time-lapse photographs are crisp and colorful scenes of the built and ruined deindustrial landscape environment, and they create both a regional sense of Camden's open and crumbling spaces, and a common space of poverty, what Vergara terms "American ruins." *invinciblecities* is striking and for me a site of longing and strange safety. The name of the site, *invinciblecities*, references the poet Walt Whitman, who lived and died in Camden, and is held within his poetics. In Camden, Walt Whitman's words are sprayed on murals, chiseled into downtown buildings, and now stuck together online.

> I DREAM'D in a dream, I saw a city invincible to the
> attacks of the whole of the rest of the earth;
> I dream'd that was the new City of Friends;
> Nothing was greater there than the quality of robust
> love—it led the rest;
> It was seen every hour in the actions of the men of
> that city,
> And in all their looks and words.[20]

Vergara's time-lapse photography in *invinciblecities* is enabled by a series of clicks on a map. The drag of a mouse moves (you) along an interactive map of Camden, and a click opens photographs that document everyday change across communities that are too often imagined as bereft of, or casualties of, history.[21] These clicks take (you to) a picture of what that single point on the map "looks" like over and in time, for example, in 1988, 2001, and 2004. The image does not stay still; it moves, changes. The mouse click is a flash. Through clicks on the website, the photos reveal themselves as constructions, the minutiae of everyday change in a neighborhood, the now-vibrant color of paint, patches of grass, old tags, and new paths.

In the distance of one of Vergara's Camden neighborhood images, filed under "decayed neighborhood," you can locate the lot at North 27th and Lincoln Avenue. In one of its incarnations, after the Mischief Night Fires of 1991, that lot was a garden. Some years after the ruins of the house were demolished and after most of the boys from our neighborhood vanished—some inside prison cells and others to early death—college students from the local branch of Rutgers University came and planted another view.[22] The lot was fenced and reimagined as a community garden project, which, I suspect, is more and more how abandoned or vacant spaces get reimagined in the ghetto, achieving futurity. As beautification, rehabilitation, and workfulness, an urban garden brings the values of productivity back into public view and casts urban youth as environmental stewards or pioneer farmers; it connects them with the ground as frontier.[23] I saw the garden for only a season. It was full of raised beds, city corn, and flowers. It was very beautiful. When I spoke to my sisters we wondered about its fate. For us, the garden was an unbelievable beauty, and it faded over a year or so, unworked. After the garden died and the lot was a place of remains once again, people began to cut through the lot to walk down the street. So many feet cut a soft footpath in the dirt. A rich and bleak reminder, maybe, of how differently people reimagine or reckon with abandonment, or that a relation with the ground is forged, made beautiful, not just with the hands that work tools, but also with running, walking, or stumbling feet.[24] In *The Lie of the Land*, Paul Carter writes:

> In wondering, and wandering, about the lost surfaces of the world, our aim is not to restore them, "landscape" them, to bring the irregular ground back into the poetic and historical picture. To restore the lost ground, as they have in the new housing estate, raising a small hill here, remarking a lost brook there, by fetishizing the environment as a concatenation of sacred groves, only contributes further to the ungrounding of the ground. Just as the bulldozer desecrated the ground, so the landscape architect resacralizes it; and neither moment, with its implicit divisions between the inside and outside, sacred and nonsacred, ever recognizes the openness of the ground, the ground as process, adjunct to walking and supporter of shadows.[25]

On February 1, 2009, a young man was shot and killed at the intersection of North 27th and Lincoln Avenue, the site of the empty lot. I was some months pregnant on that night, and just before the shot I felt the quickening, the bit of electricity that is the first felt sign of movement in utero. I went upstairs to get to my cell phone and whisper to my boyfriend all about it. And I was rocked by a gunshot blast on the other side of the window. I recall the former and latter movements and moments together, because it was traumatic. One moment props up the next. The next afternoon the young man's family came there to grieve him at this spot. He had been named Luis. He was twenty-seven years old. This is the median age in Camden, twenty-seven. I was twenty-seven when I found myself so lost that I had to come home, back to Camden to recover. He was African American and Puerto Rican, like most of the people who live in this town. That afternoon my mother walked across the street to join his sister and cousins and friends where they gathered, along the edge of that lot. I couldn't manage the walk. My mother worked as a teaching assistant at his (our) elementary school, Washington School, just around the corner, and when he was in fourth grade he had been a student in her class. He had just returned home from prison when he was killed. A little spirit house was put there, with candles and balloons, and people were drinking all day.

In wondering after the topography of an "open" ground, a repertoire of nonviolent movement, a falling, I begin again here. On that day I had just arrived home and I told my parents I thought it was time for them to get out of there. My father made a sweeping gesture and told me that all this was going to change.

You wait and see Merce. In ten years this will all be different.

I didn't say anything. But Dad was right. Ten years later and we'd all be gone. Our house boarded up. Something I could not imagine, although it surrounded us. That night the young man was shot and killed in front of my parents' house. I pulled back the curtains and saw the white mini-van idling there in the middle of the street. The lights were still on in the van, and this made it seem unreal. The fire engines were there for a long time that night. I laid next to my four-year-old son who had been asleep just above the shooting, in the bedroom I once shared with my sisters, our girlhood perch, feeling the electrical currents of another pregnancy, the room alight in the reds and oranges of silent sirens, and I watched them hose down the curb.

My father was the first to leave; in his old age war trauma gave him the urge to run. And so, he ran for a season, Spring 2010, and we couldn't find him, and he lost just about everything he had brought with him. And then everything he owned. My sisters urged our mother to leave the house and to stay with them. They were convinced that alone her movements, her comings and goings, were leaving a vulnerable and visible trail. Their house sits empty now, foreclosed. So little left to pay, but still too much. Someone stole into the basement not too long ago and took all the copper pipes. When my mother went to check on the house she was knee deep in water.

Some of my favorite words locate and join: *at, with*. You might say: *with so and so*. And *at* would tell you when or where. This is so you could know when she is coming back. Like at so and so time, so she could be at home with you. But now maybe you can't get home. Maybe your home is destroyed. But that happens there, you know (in Camden), someone can just go in and rip it all out, the precious metals. Swing a sledgehammer maybe, a chair into the walls. They will tear like paper. Extract all the copper pipes. Take them to the junkyard. For sale and meltdown! That happened at your house, when you were gone, when we were all gone, when you weren't together anymore.

So, are they still your favorite words?

Yes, I think so. They can still bring it all back.

When your house is gone, are you still gonna stay there?

Yes, I think so.

The house sits and the land shifts. How to attend to this place in the light of the kind of losses and lives lived here? Wahneema Lubiano writes that remembering is "enlarging a space where before there prevailed simply an account of ghetto violence."[26] These lots and empty houses are enlarged spaces, spaces of remembrance and everyday life—what people have been left with, to invent, survive, fight, walk, through. Invent a walk to survive what they have been through and left with.

I was looking out of windows and writing. I thought, remembered, saw, and reset things. That way. What we could lose is humbling. Turned out, seeing it all again, from the other side of property. We are boarded out of the little broken down house. Access given up or refused. But this familiar earth. It comes back to us.

My arrangements are simple. The curve of a banister when you were at the bottom of the steps, a small wooden door to the basement, an iron grate that channeled the heat through your little house. The things that kept the upstairs from the downstairs, and that kept life warm and moving between.

My little sister and I watch the oil truck (Carrion?) pull away from our curb and then make it to the wrought iron vents in time for the coming heat. It blows up our shirts and we are happy because there is oil for the month, and we balloon. When the house is empty you will want these treasures, to stash them away or drag them behind you as if feathered or winged. Here's what I bring home, what I can carry: a paint-speckled hook. Two thousand miles away I screw it to my bedroom door, to hang a collection of thrift shop purses and a silk robe.

I transfer landscapes, lay homes, that one onto this one. And when that one becomes this one I am in that other sala by the air conditioner in the window and I can almost hear the Spanish church next door where the German Maennerchor used to be. The parishioners are getting out of a service. I see the empty lot across the street, that corner. And Mom may come down the stairs and head into the kitchen. She might close the door behind her and call her mother and talk very loudly, because her mother is in Puerto Rico and she is hard of hearing now. And my dad and my son might be asleep upstairs, each in one of the two bedrooms. Or I might not have children yet. I might be going into the dining room and sleeping alone by the window in a single bed.

In neighboring Philadelphia during World War II, the *Philadelphia Record* newspaper documented public drives for the acquisition of scrap metal. The call honed individual survival practices and what is imagined as the disorganized work of the poor and disenfranchised. The call to war work and the public dumping or making of piles was integral to a nationalist project. The scrap was assembled of and comprised personal artifacts alongside impersonal public objects—"fire hydrants, musical instruments, keys"—and publicly displayed a reusable mix of useless things, knotted and untethered at memory.[27]

Recycling and scavenging are daily survival practices for people who are living on low incomes across the United States. The scrap metal industry is a site of accumulation that globally circulates the raw materials of the "inner city," the historical conditions and fallouts of deindustrialization and the materiality of disposability in Camden's built environment and its commodified scraps. Demolition and recycling are widespread in Camden, constitutive of the dispossession and unmaking of the landscapes of Camden neighborhoods, and are embedded in foreclosure and structural economic abandonment. Can an abundance of storytelling, the very minimum of memory, work against the discourses of capital accumulation, the extraction of human and raw materials, and the language of consumption and economic production?[28]

The scrap metal industry is a site of accumulation that globally circulates the raw materials of the "inner city." Today EMR, a global recycling corporation with sites in North America, Europe, and Asia, operates scrap metal depots in Camden. In addition to the four Camden Iron and Metal sites operated by EMR, multiple scrapyards in Camden are subsidiaries of EMR. Accumulation, extraction, and dispossession in the circulation of the transnational scrap metal recycling industry routes through Camden. Was this the fate of our pipes? When Mom went into the basement and the walls were torn open and the pipes were gone? Who whistled their way up the street pushing a cart or hopped into their loaded truck with all the pipes anyway? Not who, not why, but the certainty of resale and meltdown.

Cramer Hill Memories

How can space engender (shared) histories through storytelling or fashion another sense of the present? During the course of my research for this project I came across a group called Cramer Hill Memories. Cramer Hill Memories is on Facebook. The group invites people who grew up in the Cramer Hill neighborhood "primarily" during the 1950s, 1960s, or 1970s to reconnect and share their memories about living here.[29] It does not include the 1980s in its invitation, because it is a site of nostalgia. By contrast, the 1980s represent the time of Camden's full-on ruination, running counter to while engendering the time and romance of nostalgia.[30] Many of the group posts include reflections on what is remembered but no longer recognizable—empty lots, boarded-up buildings, and blocks ruined by fires and the violence of and in the city. In reading the posts—and this is why this group makes an appearance here—I discovered that the man who started the group, which was active and had more than nine hundred members at the time of my browsing, once lived in the abandoned house across the street from the house I grew up in, at North 27th and Lincoln Avenue. He and his family lived there between 1956 and 1975. In a black-and-white picture from the site, two of the family's boys sit on a sleigh in the backyard. They are bundled up and smiling, and the older boy waves. The yard is filled with snow. Here is how he captioned the picture: "This was taken in our little backyard on Lincoln Avenue in Cramer Hill. We lived on the corner of Lincoln Avenue and North 27th Street. I think I was about five years old and my brother Dan about 2 years old. We Kelleys lived at 1028 North 27th Street from 1956 to 1970. My grandmom Rachel Kelley continued to live there until she retired to Georgia in 1975. The house burned down sometime after 1985. It is an empty lot now."[31]

From Mr. Kelley's continued posts, to my great astonishment I learn that the house was once a boarding house, that this spot in the cut has been a gathering space for many kinds of arrivals, travels, crossings, and (mis)rememberings for at least one hundred years. Fred Moten writes that the ensemble as "the improvisation, rather than reading of totality, allows an accord between the ongoing and the 'to come.'"[32] I imagine the empty lot at North 27th Street as an ensemble formation, another kind of futurity "to come," an arrival that agitates against productivity.

I wonder what a repertoire of nonviolent movement can mean in Camden, New Jersey, and what it has to do with the many empty lots, at corners, between houses. Robert Beauregard notes: "When we discuss urban decline or read how others perceive it, we engage with highly charged stories built up of layers of subjective impressions, not emotionally flat renditions of objectively specified conditions. Decline involves personal and collective loss and that loss constitutes a symbolic alienation from the city."[33]

The landscape shifts in so many "across the street" and "next door" lots are most immediately related to deindustrialization, crack, and related forms of economic violence and social abandonment. These open spaces are a commons, most readily available for many kinds of everyday use, in/visible cultural practices, activities, and inventions—play, drugs, sex, parking, and revivals. In their myriad and everyday uses, the play of children and public and sexual cultures, these landscapes are leftover and wondrous.[34] The geographies of neighborhood and abandonment are complex. In Camden, site specificity is troubled, but it is a generative and creative condition. Ongoing and relational place-making movements and practices perform livable worlds.[35] Camden's vacant lots are social sites of everyday performance, landscapes remade at dispossession, abandonment, and foreclosure. Vacant lots are an index of violent crime in urban neighborhoods.[36] They are also intersections, after Caribbean theorist Sylvia Wynter, unfinished spaces, "not simply a sociodemographic location but the site both of a form of life and of possible critical intervention."[37] The empty lot across the street from what was once my mother's house is open ground. It has been a boarding house, a home, a crack house, an open space, a community garden (planted by white students from the Camden branch of Rutgers University), and a makeshift church parking lot. It swells with memories—crack and fires and lives lost to imprisonment and early deaths. These days the storefront Spanish church erected a fence around the lot again and started parking attendees' cars there and holding revivals.[38] Through loudspeakers they project song, preach, play gospel and even reggaeton. At this vacant lot I am left wondering—an open ground still so full of callings and sound; people sitting up, not on a porch now, but prayerful and singing in folding chairs. And I remember a girlhood crush who spent just about every day across the street on those steps before the 1991 fire, up and about. He addressed high school me just this once as I left the house. And he said this:

If I wasn't drinking and selling drugs I'd marry you.

And I said nothing then.[39]

On the day the remains of the house at 1028 North 27th Street and Lincoln Avenue were demolished, Mr. W. Hargrove, the owner of W. Hargrove Demolition (a company that has made a killing in this city), came to survey the job. From our porch I watched the last bits of everything buckle and fall, the stairs where the frenzied beautiful ones of my adolescence sat and smoked their weed, stashing their drugs and things in reusable brown paper bags left in the weeds growing alongside our porch. Mr. W. Hargrove tells my father that I look like a movie star, but what catches the demolition man's eye is devastation. If Camden's archives are indeed ruinous, its "vacant" landscapes are active, integral to remaking a sense of the present, legible perhaps only where the raced discourses of recovery and revitalization (ruin and redevelopment, underperformance and rehabilitation) intersect. As forms, they hold the impressions of a (once) built environment and cast possible futures.

There are stages of decline, the space before the total ruin of demolition sets in, and life is improvised at padlocked fences and boarded-up windows and doors. We watched the lot across the street from where our house sat, and where we lived, as it went through these processes. In this we all left our wonder and thoughts and dreams there too. During this time the lot was heavily attended; that is to say lots of people would gather there, in the house that was there before the fire and its demolition, when people would sit for hours and across three seasons on the outside, or slip away inside, having broken in, and do all kinds of things in there, beyond the view of the outside. I never wondered about the insides of that house, what it might have looked like, nor did I ever break in. It was the outside that fascinated me. The boys who lived all around arrived at the house as if in answer to an invitation. The house dwarfed us, as would a stage erected just before your house, set just across the street. A patchwork of green, brown, and gray wood boards covered each of its once glass windows, the design work of years of prevention and disrepair. My sisters and I watched the streets, curtained behind our bedroom windows in the middays of the summer months, when our windows stayed open and the boys called out to each other in two languages and removed their T-shirts to use them as towels and to shield their eyes and faces from the sun, as it was very hot and there was no shade at the corner. The boys used the porch for rest, and depending on the whereabouts of the sun, they sat there for some shade. During the summer months we probably watched them more intently than they watched us on our weekday walks home from the bus in the fall, because in the summer we were inside and we were perched just above them on a second floor, keeping our own privacies against the intense heat and humidity that made the stillness of hiding at the windowsill or laid out in our own underwear a strategy to endure the heat of our house. We gathered in this way and each found our ways to make use of the space, mostly as a way to come together, sit for a bit or a while if they wanted to and dream transact. They also wrote all over the house. They wrote their names, a warm impression, and a defensive architecture. The house is long gone now. We are all moved on. It is just the green grass of a small clearing and a chain-link fence, not so tall. It could still easily be hopped.

One night these boys pull a white boy out of his small white car. He has pulled up alongside them to buy the drugs they sell from this corner. Whether they know him or have a history, whether they exchanged words or slurs or just silently opened his car door and dragged him out, I cannot tell you. They pull him out from the insides of his car and they begin to beat him. He is alone. They beat him all over the head and when he falls down to the street they kick him all over his body. I watch as one boy finds a rock, debris from the side of the crumbling vacant where they do their hanging, and he brings it over and drops it on the white boy's head. I see the rock come down on this white boy and I remember it as a thing that no one objects to. That is to say, not one of the boys says no, don't do that. Maybe they are all caught up, maybe they are holding onto each other as a group and so they do not want to compromise that ethic. I do not call out from the window. I only watch as one of the boys climbs atop the roof of the white boy's car. It is the boy who has used the rock. He's just a year or two younger than me. He stands there and begins to jump up and down. Some of the boys then begin to rock the white boy's car while their friend is still on the roof. Back and forth the car rocks and the boy atop rides the wave until he jumps down and a few of them collectively turn the car over onto its side. One of the boys uses some of the debris from the house to create a fire. They torch the car and run away. The white boy is left behind and crawls to the curb. We go and wake up our father and he is so groggy from the combination of his medications. He is not meant to wake so soon, but when he sees the flames he goes on high alert. We stand at the doorway to my father's bedroom to call him. My father cannot be touched awake and says never to tiptoe around him if he is asleep. If he is awoken this way he has a Vietnam flashback, so at the threshold of his room we call out to him moderate to loudly:

Dad!

My father finds his keys and moves his car (a plain Blue Toyota Tercel hatchback that we call his shuttlecraft, as a nod to his love of Star Trek) up a few feet from where he usually parks it in front of our house. He does this so that his car does not catch fire. Dad refuses to adorn his car with Puerto Rican regalia; he doesn't want to draw the attention of the cops when he is out on the road. No one attends to the white boy who has been beaten and is lying at the opposite curb until a fire truck arrives and puts out his car and he disappears inside an ambulance.

We shake our heads and withdraw our compassion. I can hear my parents asking:

Quién te manda?

You got what you asked for or came for, and if a beating is ever a lesson. The harshness of this is set in the late night when a fire disrupted the ordinary illumination of the street lights and everyone could take no more.

Turning back. What it means to write it now, when the place of my writing is gone. I can't get in there anymore. It isn't private. It isn't ours. But it is open and boarded up now. A condemned public and a private property. Perhaps the loss, the opening, makes it all the more mine? Ours? Maybe it is more available than ever. I wrote from inside. I looked out. Now I am standing between what can seem like two vacancies, mirrored, twinned. To take memory, block by block. To linger at an empty space. To rethink a spatial imaginary at the fragments of traumatic memory. There is a sense of unison at the path, call and response between foot and land. A fine attunement to this terrain.

In 2001 at night I walk around the corner. Up and down the block. I'm walking to quiet my mind or else to outrun it. It doesn't stop. It's a freight train not a river. I ache for my old mind and ways. I smoke menthol after menthol. The neighbors down the way are out tonight too. I think they are new Dominicans. It is a warm night. Their front door is open and some people come outside; others are gathered in the living room. Besides them, it is just me. The street lights do their work against the night sky. I pull my hoodie up and make my way around the block. Just across from what was my elementary school, George Washington Elementary School, I stop and look down at the sidewalk. It is overrun with water bugs. They are everywhere. I step backward at their coming and going. I cannot believe how many there are. Seems like a thousand. They are a night lake, iridescent. I turn around and head home so as not to crush the caravan underfoot.

I can't sleep. I step out just before dawn. Quiet so I will not wake the house. On the back porch I sit and wonder whether I will ever be myself again. I smoke. I lament. It feels real. It feels like it matters. The sun doesn't rise. The birds do. The sky is their song. I hear it before I see the light. I hear a multitude of birds and they are singing and I am stilled, because who knew? I didn't know the birds did this. That they silence me, accompany me; it is a gift of a moment I cling to, even still. In Camden, when I was despairing, all this a reminder. You are not alone.

A young girl's walk to and from school. A bus ride downtown. Did that corner burn too? The source of the fires. What is the source of the fires? The building was already coming down. Our house was already coming down. Melted here and there in 1991. Inside, a hole in the roof, in the wall on the way downstairs. The sheetrock, the wood always exposed. You are never far from wear and tear—always consider the layers and insides of things—and you wonder after those things have been closed up. Then later the pipes. Torn out.

THREE

Demolition Futures

I can remember when the Riverfront State Prison was built, only because I can remember crossing the Benjamin Franklin Bridge between Camden, New Jersey, and Philadelphia. When you looked down it was there, just below the bridge, a prison in miniature. Although contested from the beginning, Riverfront State Prison was built at the waterfront in exchange for state funding. Camden's waterfront redevelopment has yet to positively impact the city's residential neighborhoods.

We did not travel much between our home in Camden to Philadelphia, mostly because we were poor and my mother did not drive, and my father was sometimes very sick. When we did travel, it was by bus, and we would wait for the "419" at the corner of River Road and North 27th Street (our block) and travel to downtown Philadelphia, which was not so far away. When we traveled by car across the bridge it was to take my father to the psychiatric ward of the Veterans Affairs hospital in center city Philadelphia (or out to the hospital in Coatesville, farther away). I and my three sisters, we'd be in the backseat of my uncle's car and we'd be equally sad and confused, and always looking out the window. Riverfront State Prison appeared to me then, as a young girl sitting high up on the bus or

3.1 Riverfront State Prison, Camden, New Jersey, 2004. Photo by Camilo José Vergara.

in the backseat of my uncle's car, as would a dollhouse, partially open and visible from above (figure 3.1).

This image of the Riverfront State Prison was taken by photographer Camilo Vergara in 2004 and was part of the *invinciblecities* website. These images were indexed, classified by census tract and theme in order to organize the viewer's experience. Some categories include decayed or stable neighborhood(s), textures of decay, postindustrial Camden, religion, people, graphics, commerce, institutions, landmarks, vegetation, fortification, things left behind, cemeteries, banks, pairs, survivors, and others. As evidenced by these categories, Vergara's Camden images move between the disorderly environment and the reconstruction of livable worlds. Yet his *invinciblecities* also creates the photograph as a chart and a map, and in this sense it is in keeping with reformist photography of urban slums.[1]

In a 2009 interview, the photographer Camilo José Vergara was asked about his Camden project:

What aspect of Camden have you yet to capture?

He responded: The future. In Camden, if this push along the water-front continues, I am really interested in the frontier. Where are they going to put the border? Because there's going to be a border. They're going to say, from here on there is middle class mixed Camden and, on the other side, here, is the ghetto. How do you consolidate that zone? You do it for one building sometimes, you can do it for the street. You can have security guards, a fenced community. Folks are thinking about it, coming up with their things, and I am out there with my camera to look and see what they come up with.[2]

In his response Vergara evokes a particular future, a city on the verge of militarization (the frontier) and segregation, and the thin veil of forti-fication that is the planning and design aspect of securitization, the mak-ing of border zones at building and street via the placement of security guards and fences.

The Riverfront State Prison was demolished in 2010. Built in 1985, it was one of the newer prisons in the state and shared the shores of the Del-aware River with the New Jersey State Adventure Aquarium and Camp-bell's Field, a minor league baseball park. The closing and demolition of the prison did not signal here an abolitionist future, but rather the re-visioning of the profitability of this industry given the conversion of the prison into real estate. The prison was torn down so that its "prime location" could be redeveloped as a tourist destination. The Riverfront State Prison Site Re-use Study featured drawings of the waterfront, reimagined as a shopping and entertainment facility.[3] Within this schema, the prison site became valuable and signaled futurity because it offered another view, away from Camden and overlooking the Philadelphia skyline. Riverfront State pris-oners were transferred to other older and more overcrowded prisons.

The reimagining of the Camden waterfront after demolition of the prison involved the use of imaginative reports, recommendations, and speculative documents—representational systems that consolidated the Camden waterfront as a border and a frontier. In 1992 the organization Save Our Waterfront grew out of local North Camden residents' active and successful opposition to the New Jersey Department of Corrections' plan to build a second prison in North Camden: "sow successfully dis-suaded the NJDOC [New Jersey Department of Corrections] from con-structing the second prison."[4] Rod Sadler, the executive director of Save Our Waterfront, spoke to a reporter writing a story about the remaking of the Camden waterfront after the prison's demolition. In his remarks, Sadler twins the desire and anxiety of a planned mixed-income community in the creation of a community whose borders do not *appear* to be closed:

> "We need to start mixing. . . . Camden people want the amenities that come from a higher-income community."
>
> The key, as always, is planning.
>
> "My son, a professor, lives in a beautiful community in Charlotte of single-family homes, cul-de-sacs, and little McMansions. . . . But on his block, there are three or four subsidized units you can't tell apart. The kids all play together. It's a positive thing."
>
> Still, Sadler realizes that well-heeled newcomers will want to distance themselves from the crime and drug-dealing in the area.
>
> "We have to make it safe," he acknowledged, "but a closed community doesn't necessarily need to look like a prison."[5]

Sadler's organization, Save Our Waterfront, and the Cooper's Ferry Development Association, a private, nonprofit corporation working in Camden since 1984—two organizations whose names interestingly articulate at once environmental and consumer claims—joined efforts to create a plan that "made sure that the North Camden Neighborhood Plan and the North Camden Waterfront Plan complement each other and that the neighborhood reconnects to its riverfront in a fun, safe, beautiful and seamless way."[6]

The Riverfront State Prison Site Reuse Study further promoted the understanding of the waterfront as frontier: "Just as the waterfront was core to the city's settlement during Colonial times and its commercial and industrial development thereafter, so does it now hold enormous potential to be a catalyst for Camden's redevelopment efforts in the 21st Century."[7]

What visions do these plans draw up and what futures do they project for the waterfront? The absence of the prison serves to tell another design story about Camden's future, to make possible the reconnection of a new community to the landscape, the waters. Drawings from the North Camden Neighborhood Plan feature a waterfront study, a green park that follows and wraps the periphery of the waters. It creates neighborhood streets as corridors that offer views of the water. The key themes of the waterfront park study included:

- Provide continuous public access to the waterfront.
- Connect the neighborhood to the river.
- Re-establish North Camden's maritime roots.
- Enhance the visual impact of the waterfront[.]
- Create a pioneering environmental education asset.[8]

Solidarity with the future, the "ensemble" of a yet-to-come, here is translated to frontier thinking, building a (housing) market economy, a population that needs to be seduced, more than building new modes of relation at and in community or communal waters.[9] Geographer Clyde Woods writes: "Throughout history, social-spatial enclosures have been used by dominant social movements to establish stable control over specific territories and their populations. This process typically involves the reorganization of property relations through the destruction of collectively held property, the commons."[10]

Camden City is overwhelmed by structural violence, and demolition is a common practice. Geographer Ruth Wilson Gilmore thinks about the "dynamic processes that renovate race and state"; in Camden the landscapes of social violence and imprisonment intersect at the discourses of demolition and reuse and renovate both race and state.[11] The demolition of the sixteen-acre Riverfront State Prison took three months. Legislation introduced by Senator Donald Norcross declared: "The New Jersey Department of Corrections has seen a general decline in the prison population. As a result, other prisons within the State system have been able to absorb transfers from the Riverfront State Prison."[12]

Drawings of the waterfront chart the forms of sanctioned movement via the built environment that create and govern waterfront views. The waterfront revitalization was expected to ameliorate the (terrifying) visuality of poverty that encompasses most of the adjoining North Camden neighborhood. Demolition was completed by Brandenburg, Industrial Service Company, a demolition company that specializes in demolition, asbestos abatement, and hazardous material removal. The prison's demolition was filmed and featured on *Mega Breakdown*, a National Geographic program that marketed the program via a spectacular discourse of recycling and punishment:

> Break It Down is tackling one of its most formidable projects ever, a
> building that was made to be virtually impenetrable ... the Riverfront
> State Prison in Camden, New Jersey. There are concrete cell blocks,

a library, a chapel, four guard towers, and razor wire—and it's all got to come crashing down. This sixteen-acre property sits on valuable riverfront real estate. So, the prison is getting a death sentence, and the land is going to be cleared for new construction. But there are obstacles at almost every turn—from the deadly risk of asbestos to the swirling snows of a winter storm. If that's not a big enough challenge, the team is working hard to recycle as much material from the old prison as they can. It's got to be carefully cleared out and shipped off, with old copper and steel becoming new products through recycling.[13]

The *Mega Breakdown* episode focused on the demolition of cell blocks, the library, chapel, and gym, and four guard towers. The prison was full of asbestos; it was behind every brick of every building and underneath the chapel floor. Recovering materials for recycling required that the walls of the building be "skinned," a process whereby the exterior of the bricks were stripped and the black asbestos removed so that the bricks would be clean for recycling. In addition to this "skinning," the stages of demolition also included extracting precious metals like copper and iron—which Brandenburg sold for company profit—and preparing for a controlled collapse. Ninety percent of the prison's structure was recycled. Things like floodlights, riot helmets, kitchen items, and toilets were warehoused for state sale. The razor wire that surrounded the prison was the last to come down; the perimeter fence that once bordered the prison now protected the company's assets, the demolition equipment and the newly acquired copper, iron, and brick, from the outlying community (of recyclers). Camden recyclers here are imagined as scavengers, and the potential theft is of raw materials. The razor wire was reused immediately to keep residents out of the site. The site, as dangerous terrain, is then protected, in case children should come to play. The recovered copper was sold and transformed into tubing for domestic plumbing. The steel was used for girders, the infrastructure of bridges. The cellblock concrete was broken down and left; it will serve as the backfill for new development at the site.

In 2012, sixty-seven people were murdered in Camden. This number holds the death of my dear Rasheeda and a boy I grew up with, Tito. Tito was the little brother of my childhood friend. Tito is shot and killed in Camden. He is thirty-three when he dies. I remember him as a little boy, running around with us when we lived at East State Street Village. His sister posts on Facebook a picture of him as a grown man. He stands with three friends. She is mourning and she writes that everyone in that picture is now dead.

A meeting in the spring of 2013, described as a trauma symposium, intended to draw attention to the violence of poverty, toward an understanding of poverty as a public health crisis.[14] The group behind this meeting, STOP (Stop Trauma on People), welcomed family members of the dead to create crosses and plant them in front of city hall to commemorate the dead, to bring the mourning wail onto the landscape. This was controversial. Politicians worried it would further bemoan the city's public image. What is the visual life of poverty in Camden? Camden's landscapes are outstanding, and people build meaningful relationships with and through their attachments to Camden's common grounds. It is a tenuous, treacherously political, movement. In 2013 I intended to travel to the symposium, but after I got off the phone with the organizer, I felt immobilized. I had a hard time getting it together to go teach. He kept saying: "You are odd. You are odd." He didn't mean this in a bad way. He meant to say, you beat the odds. You beat the odds. There is a less than 1 percent chance that a woman from Camden would earn a PhD.

Wrestling with these documents, the politics of redevelopment and revitalization, I am left wondering at how carefully the future is emptied, wrought in figures and plans, how the people of Camden, all the people, disappeared.

In spring 2015 the Camden Night Gardens festival took place on the former grounds of the Riverfront State Prison. As a project of the Cooper's Ferry Development Association's Connect the Lots Initiative, the 2015 Camden Night Gardens took the theme of "city invincible" and brought together artists and community members under Walt Whitman's call to a public expanse.[15] The theme "City Invincible" was described thus: "Symbolically rising from the rubble of the Riverfront Prison, the Camden Night Gardens is meaningfully contributing to Camden's urban renewal by restoring beauty to the waterfront, creating a platform for diverse creative expression, and attracting economic activity to the area. Drawing upon Camden's rich past and dynamic present, Camden Night Gardens is a beacon of the revitalization that can be achieved through culturally and community driven placemaking."[16]

A collaborative mural along the Delaware River spelled out "Invincible City"; a different artist designed each letter. Once taken down, the letters will be individually redistributed throughout the city as public art.

The Camden Night Gardens propose a particular view of Camden; it is cultivated at night to bear a certain message. What kind of a making is being called forth in the call to community expression via restoration of the beautiful? To "Black lite" basketball games at night between urban youth and police, or a raised platform where contemporary Camden poets can read and engage in a spoken-word battle under the banner of Whitman's legacy? The Camden Night Gardens are a call to a particular public and a making of a commons that tells about possession and visibility, that is, all the things it can mean to be a "beacon." Here, the presence of the police and the lights serve a regulatory function; one can be seen (be safe) at night. Light installations projected Whitman's verse onto Camden's existing architecture to transform the space. Unlike graffiti that may tell another kind of story, light projections offer good, clean, movement. Light was also critical to the Shadow Stage, a projection of choreographed movement and dance screened on a water tower that once sat next to the Riverfront State Prison: "The site of the water tower was previously occupied by the New Jersey Riverfront State Prison that was demolished in 2010, thanks to a broad coalition of Camden citizens. Turning the water tower into a monumental screen for the play of light and shadow, the music and dance performances will powerfully animate this site of a historic victory that demonstrated the power of the Camden community when mobilized."[17]

The display and projection was made testament to a "historic victory," the collective action that took place to bring the prison down. The discourse of demolition as abolition, however, serves to mask a project of revitalization, a perhaps clearer function of the shadow in the project.

Assembly and trespass are key modes of democratic and protest behavior. The Night Gardens provides an idea of Camden; however, it may be that the opportunity for assembly is just a rehearsal of the arts, a usable expression that "attracts economic activity to the area." It may be that other sounds and venues—long gone, coming, unheard. Between the sounds of young girls who shriek and train themselves to silence and sound, or where representation can fall away, more closely aligned as it is to the real. To disassemble the setup of art as beauty, the grounds of a new kind of being, one that breaks from real estate and revitalization at any and all costs.

As the city's most visible and wavering symbol of revitalization, the waterfront is a valuable site of economic accumulation, a place of relation where fictions of community are staged and divided. In *Abolition Democracy* Angela Davis underscores the forms of violence "linked to the practices of imprisonment and the circuits of violence linked to one another."[18] She says the prison appears and disappears as an absent presence. This is the case in Camden, where the future is so often represented as speculative, a frontier. Camden's landscapes are rich, beyond proximity to Philadelphia, which is always an approximation of, and to, a particularly empty staged future. Residents build and move meaningfully along Camden's landscapes. Camden's borders, at the waters, are contested, future grounds. The violence of disappearance plagues Camden's residents, who are subjected to everyday forms of terror and state violence. The Riverfront State Prison was instructive: it made punishment visible on the landscape, and it was there to terrorize the people incarcerated within and the residents just outside. When the prison came down, a park was planned, and then, too, the gardens, to offer corridors and light, a spatial imagination of a view, a spell, and a sanctioned path to renewal and movement.

At the Walter Rand Transportation Center, I watch the 452 NJ Transit bus pull away and I know I'm in for a wait. That was my bus. I don't bother crossing against a red light or trying to signal the driver so that I might board. A friend once told me, never run for the bus. I tend to heed this advice, even though I'm in Camden. The bus shelter benches are pretty full, so I stand in the corner shade of a small tree. Lots of people are waiting for the bus this morning: mothers, fathers, grandmothers, grandfathers, sons, and daughters of all ages. And while some come and go, others kind of just hang out. When I return to the Transportation Center four or so hours later that afternoon, some of these folks are still here—some of the waiting that comes alongside selling drugs and sex work at a bus depot.

When my dreams are disturbed they are set on our block, sometimes inside or outside of our house, and there are wayward buses, strangers, tilted floors, and warehouse or prison hallways. And when the dreams collect I am afraid to come home, to Camden. Between an intense morning heat, my own remembrances, and the pleasure fade of bus stop pimping, I find myself tripping. I pick away at the open-faced cruelty of a black eye and a few too-thin women. I wonder at a crisis of relations, my own. Upset in public when I was a young girl and I'd wait at bus stops or walk with my older sister home from school or from our every-other-Saturday job of helping our mom clean the church. Men on foot, or on bikes, or in their cars would stop us. My sister would smile and kind of shake her head no. I'd glare and my sister would get mad at me and tell me to act cool, because you cannot upset them or meet their aggression. She was trying to protect us by smiling. Behind sunglasses this morning I'm sadder and grown, but I feel some of the way I felt then, when I tried to balance an excess of feeling with just how much I wanted to recede. I think we have all this in common.

At the local branch of the Camden Public Library, which was housed in a small building near to where we lived for a time on Yorkship Square, I was desperate to check out a book, a pop-up book. The library only had one, though, and it was either a popular children's checkout or delinquent, because it took a very long time to get back to the library. By the time I got my hands on it, I was very disappointed. It was about rockets, something I had no interest in at the time. When on a bus ride through downtown I discovered the Camden Free Public Library, a large and stately Carnegie library, I was all a-wonder. If we could just get off the bus and go in, linger and look, check out the library and check out a few books. Years later, in a book by the photographer Camilo José Vergara, I would finally see the insides of the Camden Free Public Library, and it was a ruin. While I wondered, a child on the outside, a tree grew up quietly past the staircase and came crashing through a hole in the roof.

The air-conditioned bus is a relief and I find myself feeling foolish. I sit back and stare out the window. Everything old is older (not just me). I call my mother from my cellphone. To tell her I've come back and to make sure I'm on the right bus. She is so happy to hear from me. She is tickled that I am on the bus and she wants to know whether I am going by the house. It is empty now. I don't know what I am in for, but I am.

I get off the 452 at River Road, just across the street from Ricardo's Pizzeria in Cramer Hill. That familiarity, an early morning blue sky, and a slip of moving clouds just above us all here this morning is enough, and I fall into the sound of my mother's laughter and a surprisingly bright reassurance that I am home. Folding this all up: the streets you knew as a girl from walking home a couple of different ways, the taste and joy of Ricardo's, and the bricks and the buildings here at this moment.

I stop in at a Puerto Rican restaurant on River Road for a snack. The alcapurria de yuca is filled with ground beef, and the lady behind the counter is warm and she asks me if I live around here as she gets me the bathroom key. I tell her I grew up here, that I lived a couple of blocks away and around the corner. My Spanish would wobble too much to say what I would think is true, but it would be something like: my parents moved away a couple of years ago now, they didn't really move though, they went separately, because my dad was so sick and he went on a disastrous run, and my mom eventually decided that she couldn't stay here without him, and she had to let go of the house to be with my dad, although it still pains her. She isn't one to walk away. I've always come home to Camden though, and now I've come home again. I'll see the house (even though it has been boarded up, because someone broke in, and it is mostly empty except for the last things in the basement, and it is going to ruin). I'll walk along Harrison Avenue.

But it would be a mistake to say all that in response to her question do you live around here? I should say, I am from here and I wonder here.

I come back here to stand at the opposite house now, with all the sounds of the day and the wind through the trees, to think through memory, to walk with multiple times of the now, to choose this as a mode of movement.

At North 27th Street, I walk across the street from our house, building an opposite safety; I am here, I am not there. I'll look over at our house from this vantage point, my back against the fenced lot. The house looks so small and clean. The Mennonite church next door probably keeps up the grounds. It is all still so alive. This fills me with surprise and a simple and stupid kind of happiness. Downstairs, the boarded up windows are covered over with a thin layer of cement. One window says, "Operation Safe Neighborhood." A large peace sign is stamped below it, and this peace sign almost looks cute, like a slogan you'd see on a shopping bag at a store marketing toward young girls. I search the windows downstairs for any sign of the bullet hole that claimed the life of my cat when I was a freshman in college, home for my first visit, but it is invisible now, the window screens covered by the wood and the cement. The railings are still intact, a small border that separated our porch just a bit from the sidewalk.

Alone, I do not cross the street or venture onto our porch. When we are gone. Our house appears to me as a small object. I wonder after the condition of its insides. Wonder after the damage. What has been taken? Metals, yes, but wood? I think about the doors and the small decorative things, the way the bannister ended in a flourish, the farmhouse door into the kitchen that was split so you could peek through the middle to spy on your mother crouched on the newspapered floor as she took a hammer to a coconut to make candy at Christmas.

By myself now, I stand across the street at the fence where I would have never stood before, because of some of the things that went down there that I could remember. When the fence went up it closed off the empty lot that many people used to cut across, a soft dirt footpath worn into patchy grass. I stood there then and heard our old across-the-street neighbor, my father's only neighborhood friend. He's always outside and talks Spanish and his voice is super gruff and loud, but he's warm. When I look on from there, at the little house, what's not our house anymore, boarded up neatly, I think about how I never stood here before. It wasn't safe and I remembered things that went down there, so I didn't go there. But here I am now, and it feels a little less than what has happened, what keeps me across the street from 1029 now.

Number 1029 was my grandmother's house. In the 1970s a lot of our family lived here. Not just my sisters and my parents, but my aunts and uncles and all their dogs. My family had the living room. I don't remember this, because I was a toddler. We slept on the floor and my mother tells me she was very miserable. Her breathing changes when she says this. I can imagine her then, always so beautiful, put upon by her children and the big personalities that pepper my father's family, and these circumstances. She says she took refuge in her mind. In her own stories. She carried this practice migrating from a girlhood in rural Puerto Rico to the shock of a Lorain, Ohio, winter in 1953.

During some of the 1980s, when all her children had moved on with their families and she had the house all to herself, my grandmother operated a small sewing operation in this living room, dining room, and downstairs in the basement of this house. She would yell at my sisters, and me, not monstrously, to get off the railing if she saw us hanging off the porch. We were really skinny kids, but maybe she thought our collective weight might eventually bring down the porch. When our grandmother moved away, my parents left the low-rise projects on East State Street and we moved in and the house became ours and the porch and its railings took on another life. We'd lean, pull, and hang together, and call out to our now-moved-away grandmother.

When I was about the age my own daughter is now, my mother would wake us up to get me and my three sisters ready for school. She'd walk us down Harrison Avenue, from our home in the low-rise projects of East State Street Village, to my father's mother, my grandmother's neighborhood in Cramer Hill. My mother used my grandmother's address so that we could go to the elementary school around the corner from my grandmother's house. At the time a schooling desegregation campaign in Camden aimed at redistributing Puerto Rican and African American kids, shuffling us around and between a few elementary and middle schools. Elsewhere this might be considered a crime, using what is called a fake address to get your kid into a school, and so my mother's going to have to line up with the other mother thieves. My mother was also working under the table, sewing piecework at my grandmother's house with a bunch of other women her age and the age of my grandmother. We were all living on welfare, but it wasn't enough. So, my mother worked under the table and didn't report the income. It still wasn't enough.

My grandmother's sewing shop was not the kind where she might measure you for a dress and then sew it, as she had once done for her own children and later for her son's marriage to my mother, sewing twelve little pink dresses for the girls who would escort my mother down the aisle to marry my dad, freshly back from Vietnam. Instead, my grandmother cleared out the furniture and purchased and set up a few large factory-style sewing machines and hired some ladies, my mother included, to work at sewing piecework. My mother worked here to supplement our family's income, before the doctors at the VA diagnosed my father, when we were still surviving on welfare and food stamps. Middle-schoolers at the time, my oldest sisters helped out there, too, after school, and earned themselves a bit of cash. A mountain of oddly shaped brown fabric rose in each corner, as my mother sewed the pieces that would make up the shoulder or arm of some still unassembled uniform. At times they stored what they'd done or what was still to be done in trash bags in the backyard. This was for safe-keeping and in case a social worker should come knocking. The backyard would appear as if it were crowded with trash, but inside the bags were the polyester uniforms that would make their way to some other worker somewhere in the world. We'd go to my grandmother's house after school, smell the coffee and chemical fabrics and her two little dogs, and wait not so patiently for our mother to be done. I'd hang on my mom's arm as she sewed, pushed rough cloth under the needle, and I'd ask her (not very nicely) to hurry up. And when she finally finished her work, placed a little cover over the sewing machine, we'd walked down Harrison Avenue, our hands dirty with educational and welfare fraud, past the Harrison Avenue landfill back to our home at the East State Street Village projects.

We'd walk each way carefully, because there was no sidewalk then and the greenery of the dump creeped out. And this is the first time I remember my mother cursing in English, a fuck! One cold morning when she was angry at the world, at my father who was home and 100 percent chance asleep. The man wasn't well. And he was younger then than I am today, but war-torn from Vietnam, and so I think I only still partially understand him, but I think I finally understand my mother.

Harrison Avenue was overgrown then, lush, green, like a wilderness, and it held for a child like me what seemed a thousand secrets: What's in there? What happened there? What is on the other side? What Harrison Avenue was, was a landfill and a toxic dump. A toxic dumping ground at the edge of the Delaware River, where the Delaware and Cooper Rivers meet, and overlooking the Philadelphia skyline. So much history there. Histories of refuse and transport, of things and people, of people made things, captive Africans in the new world, whom slavers sold here, at Petty's Island in the middle of the Delaware River, to avoid paying taxes in Philadelphia. I did not know this then. I didn't realize we were bordered by so many ancestral African American histories and so much flight, so much water. What would this knowledge have meant for me then? To know and imagine along the histories of those waters?

The Delaware River was a site of transit, a port and marketplace for the sale of captured African people into slavery. In November 2017, members of the Middle Passage Ceremonies and Port Markers Project: Remembering Ancestors (MPCPMP) erected a small memorial to signal and commemorate the passing and passage of millions of Africans into new-world slavery, and to mark one of the sites in Camden where they were made to disembark and were separated again from their relations, from the people they may have forged fugitive relationships with onboard ships. From the Middle Passage to the shorelines and grounds of Camden, the marker denotes a cultural geography, a site-making project of conversion, and a human being and her energies become laboring object and racial capital. The 2017 ceremony was attended by residents, the named and unnamed descendants of enslaved Africans, and New Jersey politicians. Libations were poured and prayers were spoken in a few languages to honor the dead. Local Camden schoolchildren read aloud the names of each African nation to underscore the vastness of the named and mapped continent and the destruction of descent, the knowledge of kin and knowledge of ancestral place, one's points of origin.

As of this writing I have yet to visit the cast-iron sign. In pictures it is painted in blues and greens. Its gold letters announce: "Enslaved Africans Once Sold Here." What follows on the small plaque, mounted high enough to be read when you stand back or crane your neck, is a short paragraph that indicates a history of American slavery. The African arrivals left no artifacts here, but this monument to the memory of them and the work of their descendants (to remember) is a call to a public memory and a memorial. What does it do to the built landscape to plant a memorial of iron and painted letters (a thing that cannot grow, that will erode, that looks back), and what kinds of visitations will it bring across the times of generations and seasons? Pictures are taken at the ceremony of children, the great-great-greats that are a trace of some of the lives that were forced into the entry, passed into the landed threshold of new-world slavery in Camden. The now reaches back, not just in memory or imagination, but across several landscapes, across people and across bodies, as the sites in Camden join a collection, a series of landscapes mapped as points along the MPCPMP that documents Middle Passage sites along the Eastern Seaboard and Gulf Coast of the continental United States. This project will install markers and make a ceremony to remember the millions of dead. In Camden, this marker is the first of three. Thus far on the map there are fifty locations, each delineated by the name of the place and a letter code:[19]

B Ports where a marker has been placed and a ceremony has been held
M Ports where a marker has been placed
C Ports where a ceremony has been held
N Ports with neither a marker nor a ceremony

At the 2017 ceremony in Camden, Senators Cory Booker and Donald Norcross sat, spoke, and extended a strong arm of politics, a public recall that may or may not correspond to the many ways they choose to inwardly make or disarticulate meaning. At the time of its installation, the Camden memorial was brought into comparison with the removal of confederate monuments across the public landscape. Some who were present and interviewed referenced a white supremacist march in Charlottesville, Virginia, and the need for a more truthful rendering of the United States and its histories of white supremacy, whereas others focused their remarks on the need to commemorate ancestral survivals. The marker is consistent with multiple meanings, as it is swept into the battle for representation and historical monumentalization. When one reads about the ceremony, it would seem that this was a part of the narrative reckoning with the politics of memory and the politics of a usable landscape that may actually elide discussions of a socio-spatial history in Camden that continues to be organized by the set of relations inaugurated at the ports of the Middle Passage, the many seasons of African arrivals. One of the uses of the marker here will be as a coordinate, one of three landing points in Camden. It seems fitting to enact ceremony here, to pour libations, words meant to reach ancestors, the gods, even still and always. The story of the day, however, does not tell of the present-day structures that have kept the descendants of African slaves enclosed or running across Camden's histories and landscapes. This may not be a point for some, nor the time and place, but it must be an axis of justice in order to unlock the potential of our histories toward a more complete emancipation and abolition, and if energy cannot be destroyed, only transfigured. What can knowledge of slavery mean toward a Black future, as kindled liberatory energy? There are pictures of the people gathered, and we can imagine how they make meaning and memory in Camden in 2017 at the placement of a marker where Black lives were commodified. I've seen these kinds of markers at heritage sites across South Jersey. Here, too, we can turn the fullness of the landscape, built, natural, to reckon with the persistence of slavery, its aftermaths, the politics of commemoration that may bracket and unsee a Black present in Camden that is still encumbered by that same violence, the socio-spatial relations of the ghetto, the becoming racial capital and the emergent socio-spatial relations that continue to structure Black life in Camden.

From Leslie Marmon Silko's novel *Ceremony*: "'They keep us on the north side of the railroad tracks, next to the river and their dump. Where none of them want to live.' He laughed. 'They don't understand. We know these hills, and we are comfortable here.' There was something about the way the old man said the word 'comfortable.' It had a different meaning—not the comfort of big houses or rich food or even clean streets, but the comfort of belonging with the land, and the peace of being with these hills.'"[20]

On May 18, 2015, President Obama visited Camden, New Jersey, to do the "unthinkable."

He held the city and its people "up as a symbol of promise." Given a new model of community policing that hinges on building communal trust and surveillance, the presidential visit significantly coupled a tour both of the Camden police force's Real-Time Tactical Operational Intelligence Center (to view the television monitor feeds of "Eye in the Sky" street surveillance cameras) and of the Salvation Army's newly built Ray and Joan Kroc Corps Community Center in the Cramer Hill neighborhood, where he delivered his remarks. In his focus on Camden, the President's remarks brought in places "*like* Baltimore and Ferguson." From Obama's remarks:

> And in some communities, that sense of unfairness and powerlessness has contributed to dysfunction in those communities. Communities are like bodies, and if the immunity system is down, they can get sick. And when communities aren't vibrant, where people don't get a sense of hope and opportunity, then a lot of times that can fuel crime and that can fuel unrest.[21]

As stand-ins, these cities are reduced to representational metaphor, and structural oppression, the ongoing historical conditions and fallout of deindustrialization, police violence, environmental racism, and distinct regional histories, are replaced by a pained body and undone senses, where only the cultivation of benevolent feelings and trust-building can cure what amounts to feeling bad. Indeed, in the President's remarks, trusted relation and benevolent feeling can emerge from a deeper policing, and surveillance figures as the safe outdoors. He elides the real Black body, the body vulnerable that cannot be recuperated, the police killing of Mike Brown. "Fuel" becomes this thing that emerges from people; their lost hopes "fuel crime, fuel unrest." Here, fuel, that toxic substance, comes from people. That Obama delivered this speech, at the site of a former toxic dump—where things like fuel, real fuel and shit, solid waste, industrial waste, methane gas, made it unsuitable for life—displays the rhetorical force of capital's imagination and reveals the materiality of vulnerability and disposability and the business of language. Given the Kroc Center's mission to focus on underserved communities and shape community wellness and legible gathering and self-improvement, President Obama calls forth in his Camden remarks the return of "able-bodied men" and "intact households." He tries to balance the weight of incarceration and policing and the fragility of a peoplehood housed in distinct familial formations and useful "able" bodies, bodies that are good for capitalism, bodies that can appear and from whom work can be extracted, houses that are "structured" and that do the work of the state.

Located on twenty-four acres at the eighty-five-acre site of the toxic former Harrison Avenue Landfill, an urban brownfield, the Ray and Joan Kroc Community Center (named for McDonald's restaurant founder Ray Kroc, and his wife's $54 million donation to the Salvation Army) includes a day care center, health center, indoor and outdoor sports facilities, and a pool; it also hosts summer camps. Imagined as the restoration of environmental relation and a reclamation of once-contaminated land, the brownfield restoration reinscribes extraction and accumulation as capital progress and accompanies the Kroc Center's underlying message of Camden's social degradation and moral composition, the materiality of vulnerability and disposability.

The City of Camden operated the Harrison Avenue Landfill as a municipal landfill from 1952 to 1971; it began to close in accordance with regulations from the New Jersey Department of Environmental Protections, but then it never fully closed, because of budget constraints. The Cramer Hill riverfront neighborhood that borders the Harrison Avenue Landfill, now the Kroc Community Center, is visibly decayed. The industrial uses along the back channel of the Delaware River restricted public access to the riverfront, and many of the residential blocks bordering the area show even higher rates of dilapidation and vacancy. From the Cramer Hill Redevelopment Study: "Industrial portions of the Cramer Hill neighborhood represent, in fact, a complete lack of use since these lands are entirely undeveloped and serve no productive use. Thus, there is no discussion as to whether or not this is the optimal use, since essentially vacant lands contain no use at all."[22]

The Cramer Hill neighborhood's waterfront accessibility and imagined stability has long made it a target of white supremacist redevelopment campaigns that hinge on eminent domain and are constitutive of the dispossession and unmaking of the landscapes of Camden neighborhoods. What might it mean to dwell at a different meaning of Camden's unthinkable, its vacant lands? To push against what Christina Sharpe defines as "salvage accumulation, the creation of capitalist value from non-capitalist value regimes"?[23] What might be an expression of comfort and peace in the very terrain marked as civilization's end? In an interview about her novel *Salvage the Bones*, Jesmyn Ward discusses the slippage between salvage and savage:

> The word salvage is phonetically close to savage. . . . It says that come hell or high water, Katrina or oil spill, hunger or heat, you are strong, you are fierce, and you possess hope. When you stand on a beach after a hurricane, the asphalt ripped from the earth, gas stations and homes and grocery stores disappeared, oak trees uprooted, without any of the comforts of civilization—no electricity, no running water, no government safety net—and all you have are your hands, your feet, your head, and your resolve to fight, you do the only thing you can: you survive. You are a savage."[24]

When I began to think through Camden I never intended to write "about" environmental fallout or imprisonment. Imprisonment, no. I was petrified of the prison and the jail in Camden, and I didn't think I knew anything about the environment, not my territory. The work started in love and in knowing that something had happened to us here and that I felt devoted to that idea and this place and its people; I had to write here. Starting there, in community and in a kind of love, I arrived at these issues and politics, which were of course there all along. This has been my route.

Twelve thousand children live in the Cramer Hill and North Camden neighborhoods surrounding the Kroc Community Center. There are differential risks in human experience and vulnerability to toxin exposure, and a game is played at what is or is not considered toxic, and for what purposes, and how to measure acceptable limits in the discourse of urban brownfield redevelopment. Brownfield redevelopment, too, articulates at once conservation and economic goals—how to relieve low income and minoritized population exposures to contamination and 'generate profit' for economic stakeholders."[25] Geographer Clyde Woods asks: "Are these communities fragmenting because they are on the margin of civilization or is it because they are on the front lines of globalization and a global racialization?"[26] The children in this neighborhood will be routed outdoors where they can be properly seen and known. Instead of running around the overgrowth of brush at what was once a dump, wasted with buried industrial by-product and shit, now they will run through the overgrowth of the Goodwill Industries. I wonder what knowledge of the waters, and the histories of the dump—where flight and fragment meet—will do for them?

The Harrison Avenue Landfill cleanup project extracted buried waste. When my dad was home asleep he was filled with Agent Orange, his inner thighs were alight, a rash of red bumps on his skin and a baseball-size tumor in his jaw and a testicle lost the same way. Dad was disfigured and then refigured by the chemical toxins of war. Who is the able-bodied man? Where is he? Vulnerable, my father was lying down, and his girls, too, walked to school this way, passing the dump, what is now a center with a rehabilitative call, to make an able-bodied child.

The lot, a potential, a boundary space for imagination and memory. A wondering. About radical change, turnings, or the slow debris of that. A turning toward itself, a piece of land, of earth; what was assembled there is now coming undone. The story of the new. A centering of a new imaginary that breaks from the old—because it must tell a particular story about the old, offer a critique and a new configuration of being, an orientation away from a particular past. It wears the guise of healing, calls itself renewal, faith, fitness. It assembles itself in eco-friendliness and foregoes a relationship with earth. The plot of earth. It may be embodied in a cross that tells you to drop your cares and worries but remakes a landscape in case you can't forget or forego. A place of a new aesthetic, the gymnasium, chapel lobby, in all a fitness club that is glass ensconced. Do all the Kroc Centers look the same? Ana remembered me. She was one of a few women working the reception counter. I walked in off the street, unsure and curious. We greet with the general warmth of strangers, but then a thread emerges, and she looks at me more closely and she asks:

Mercy?

She really saw and remembered me before I really saw and remembered her, and then I see her for real and I am moved and struck with the warmth of knowing you will be well met. When I was a teenager in the Spanish Baptist church, Ana arrived. She was beautiful and maybe a decade older than me, a young Puerto Rican woman with that golden skin and reddish hair. It has been more than twenty years since I saw her, since I went to church. She takes me around, opening doors, giving me a tour of the facilities, as we reach back into other memories, and make our way around the center.

One axis of the care offered (to be taken up or emanating like a beacon) at the Kroc Center, articulated at Obama's visitation ceremony, and like the care from the Camden Coalition of Healthcare Providers, may be to channel energies that have the potential to undermine the wellness or construction and constitution of the building itself, and toward productive values and an interiority that works away from the street. It is a project that reinvests in the power of people by channeling human energies into a value stream that will reduce cost, remake, and hold a neighborhood in its image.

But to remember here, not to habituate, but rather to enjoy and will other pasts, other possibilities for the past, into a future that is not beholden to an empty or state-sanctioned narrative of our histories or cultural practices. To remember here to serve a redress in Camden for the land, the air, the deliberate movements of people throughout that are akin to those places and scenes.

Memory, too, may be a call to witness that does not service or escort a punishing justice inside. Wind is in the trees, the matter of this place—cast-off things, things hung out on a fence to dry, Dad's grease rags fallen from the porch, toys left on the grass—they are in full bloom, a chorus, a social life, our things outside, we, however, whatever aesthetic, the life of us then, there, now.

FOUR

Halfway
Houses

I stopped watching HBO's show *The Wire*. I was warned about the scene of the detectives finally getting to the vacants, breaking open the wood-shuttered doors and windows to find all the missing bodies (the ones no one was really looking for); I thought that would be the scene to do me in. Not the gruesomeness of decomposition or the body count, but the house itself—it would become our house, our neighborhood, our Camden, and it would be too much for me to bear. My breathing changed and I felt terrible as the nails came undone and the detective opened it up, but I kept watching.

I stopped watching *The Wire* when the character named Body got killed. It did something to me. The "hopper" boy who grows up all of a sudden, and he's still young, but worn out, ashen, and tired. He doesn't wear his clothes like he used to, the do-rag either, and everything on him betrays his insides, a relentless tiredness. This may be natural, the staleness of getting older and looking at one's life from another vantage. He's too old to be a corner boy. He can see that this isn't going to pan out. He's talking to the cops. He's lost the territory and protection of the low rises. The Barksdale family. He refuses to run and gives up while he's standing.

He's gunned down on the corner by a rival up-and-coming group and he dies. I cut the TV off and didn't watch any more episodes.

I had not seen a show that reflected that low-rise project terrain. In Camden we used to live in East State Street Village, later called Centennial Apartments. Behind our apartment, which felt really big—two floors, three bedrooms—was a large field. Far off at the edge it was bordered by a line of vacant apartments, some just empty, others destroyed. They formed a little chain. My sisters and I played there constantly, in the field, and sometimes we'd threaten the youngest that we'd take her over there, to those houses at the edge, and leave her out there alone. The landscape of our play was bordered by a vacant and empty row, and for us it was a place of imaginary power and punishment. We weren't far off.

W. Kamau Bell, a comedian and host of the CNN show *United Shades of America*, is in conversation with his audience and riding along with a Camden police officer while shooting an episode of his show. Bell is a stand-up comedian who is investigating a new community policing model the city of Camden has rolled out. His show starts with Bell on stage, holding court with the people assembled in the audience. Then the show cuts to the field. On a crisp sunny day, they respond to a call, Bell and the policeman he is shadowing. Some people are using a vacant house as a place to shoot up. The viewing audience sees some of them, a few youngish but tired-looking white boys sitting on the porch of this vacant row home. They have been caught—buying, using, selling? I can't recall whether this is made clear, but they are busted. Bell speaks to a midlife (maybe) Puerto Rican man who lives in the neighborhood. The man is so tired of this kind of use of the house. He's got kids. He's a father and his kids play outside here. We see a basketball hoop, probably made from a milk crate. So, this gives us the impression that some real (want of) play is going on here in the street. Some real invention. The guys on the porch, the father, they are all kinds of desperate, but between the TV cameras and Bell, maybe some of this evaporates a bit and it has got a reportage feel or—.

An older Black woman in good spirits drives by. Bell stops her to talk. She answers his questions from inside her car. He wonders at her general good mood and the casual entrance of her car by or into what for him is an extraordinary scene. Like, how can this be normal? It is the character of the house itself that seems to push Bell over the edge of perception, to where he begins to cry (if crying is over the edge). The side of the house.

Bell is a comedian and when he watches, observes—that is to say, when the camera shifts and we are made to observe the side of the house—we see the gape. The side of the house is gone. A crumble. The house stands on what seems like three walls and a porch. It was a row house. It's not a row anymore, but you can see that it was in the way these Camden houses send out a lonely call. The house is open on one side. Bell imagines his kids playing (being children in a state of imagined childhood), and he himself begins to break down (if that is what crying is, a small break that is headed down). Eventually, he goes in. Bell and the camera go inside of the house. He points out that this was once somebody's home. You can see that quality of homefullness in the choice of carpet, of the things that still adorn the house. A plush red-maroon carpet was made for toes and people who may love gatherings and definitely love each other; it defines the deep vibrancy of privacy and décor. This is some of what the things inside the home begin to show us: that the home now serves as temporary shelter, that folks might trip out or fall asleep here now in some type of drug reverie, thinking or feeling deeper things, surface things, the kinds of things that pass for all of us at home sometimes, but the show won't muse. Maybe because Bell is rolling with the police today, and all of this is under the banner of some form of policing and criminalized behaviors— trespass, drug use. Not our trespass or the camera's trespass. Still, he shows us some kind of underlying grief that policing, camera, narrative do not resolve. It is what everyone gathered there has in common.

You might go to a house like this one—busted—and try to feel something or feel no thing and then there, in there, you might find enough room for all of what you need at that moment too. Or maybe you see a few things there that make you know you can return. Someone else's stuff, touch of life, helps you, supports you in your ways, habits. Habitual. Inhabit. Inhabit. To live. Keep some of these things. They are useful—say carpet, say porch, say exit through the broken wall. What made this place inhabitable?

The open house. The things on display. No longer touchable. The presence and absence of the vacant on the landscape. That they should bear study, a study in relation, the character of a place. Not in the repopulation of individual life, lives. Here, a memory, an opening, a collective? The comings and goings of many. People at the openings. The long or only recently gone.

Mr. H spends time outside then goes to meetings in the neighborhood that are about the neighborhood. Once, he seemed to run Lincoln Avenue, the block that intersected with our house. He ran his sons and some of their friends or boys their age. They ran the drugs and occasionally they used the side of our house to stash stuff in little brown bags.

Mr. H rode a bike up and down the block. A small BMX-type bike. He cruised along. Rode up and down and in circles. Surveying the movement of the boys, his stuff, maybe remembering his days as a boy himself, in rural Puerto Rico, where, my father tells me, his own father made him sleep in a small cage. Is my dad pulling my leg? Many years after, he softens up and gets back to church. He is an old man now. Mr. H comes over and drinks coffee on the porch or inside in the sala. And if I'm home I usually retreat to the kitchen or upstairs. It is my general shyness, but, too, it was harder for a while for me to shake my idea of Mr. H as a grandmaster drug lord. My dad shakes it. They are brothers in Christ. But I remember being stuck inside because Mr. H and his boys, sometimes a dozen or more in the flock, were outside stopping cars. They stopped every car that slowed on our street. When it was us, when a car pulled up to drop us off, the boys would gather with the line:

What you need . . . oh.

They'd see us and back up. A look. They never said anything back. No fights. Some things trump a transaction. The swirl of our embarrassment and annoyance, all that we felt, our temporary confusion and recognition, us all being the same age.

Prison Street! Prison Avenue!

The Puerto Rican guy crossing midstreet and against the light loudly calls out. And then he's a town crier; there is joy in his critique, and it blasts through the January snow at the confusion of M. L. K. and Mickle Boulevards.

You aren't from around here are you? It was a school. Now it's the YMCA. (When I point and ask him what that building is over there, the one facing the jail. I stopped him as he was jumping into his car to drive away.)

He calls me out before he answers my question. And so, I say I am.

I am, but it's been a long time.

Oh. You got a boyfriend?

I walk away speaking.

Yeah I do, in California.

Well you don't have one out here.

One is enough.

Our laughter, as we exit. Him, he goes into his car and I, I go to my appointment at the Walt Whitman House, which stands just behind us, cradling our exchange.

The Camden Free Public Library at Federal Street in downtown Camden is in the cut, just against the prison and the Camden County Hall of Justice. It is closed down. Lots of books sit on the shelves. The shelves appear to be full. The patron tables are set with books, but the library is shut down. A thickish layer of dust covers the tabletops, and yet as far as library scenes go, it looks very much alive. Like people were just here and they had to step out or someone is giving a lunchtime reading in another room just past our view from the window where we peer in, and they've all run off to see her, but they'll come back, so they've left their books on the table. The library has been closed for some time. I ask two corrections officers walking in the alley that adjoins the library and the jail.

How long has the library been closed?

Seven years.

He chuckles at me.

The other says: There are libraries in Centerville and Cramer Hill, but no, none downtown anymore, as far as I know.

I point to the library.

All the shelves and tables are still set.

The laughing one says: If you care so much about the books you should contact City Hall and see about getting them donated.

The woman must see my face, because she says: Maybe to the jail?

I go back to loitering at the picture window.

I write from a picnic bench. We are just one day outside of the snow and extreme cold that has had me locked down for the past couple of days, and I am on foot. But it has warmed up. I'm writing outside in the plaza of the Maria Barnaby Greenwald Camden County Hall of Justice, dedicated May 1996. I would have liked to write from inside the library. To go in there, settle down at a table, surrounded by the books, and to write. But it seems I am foiled again. I forgot that the libraries bore the heat of a fiscal crisis.

Walt Whitman's House is all a wonder. Whitman's room, he kept all those papers scattered about, piles and piles of paper, his papers. The curator says they cleaned up a bit for the old photograph they took of Whitman's stuff. Still a mess though. I'm struck by the similar scenes of literacy and love. Here and then over at the Camden Public Library. One is carefully curated, beloved objects set, and one is a scene of crisis and abandonment. And yet set here, the Whitman House will tell this story too.

The library's entrance is blocked by somebody's stuff, sleeping bag or blanket, a bottle of juice, all covered over by a large clear plastic tarp to keep their things together and dry, because it has been snowing and they have been going it, life, outside.

Whitman's bed made the rounds before it was finally returned to the museum-home. The bed he died in, six-foot-two-ish, shrunken a bit by old age and illness. The narrow stairs he was carried down.

I cannot get up close to the window on one side of the library because the person's stuff is in the way, and even though we are outdoors and the person isn't here right now, I don't want to step over someone's space and things.

The house-museum is a jewel. It opens up like a locket. Inside is a warm light and I'm aglow.

I'd wanted to make my way home, back to the house that was ours, when we were all together and I could come home and be with them, but after seeing the library I am feeling so disappointed. The Whitman House lit me up inside. Bright! Bright! At the library, I crashed a bit. And that little crash is just enough, and I can't carry myself home, to our empty, boarded-up house today.

I suppose I could write that they are similar. Come to a standstill. A closing.

Here's what gets me about the library. It is not boarded up. You can still look through the windows and see into the inside, you can see all the books. Some books are stacked on and stranded at the tables. I spot Amy Tan. Some videos are still on the shelves. I spot a documentary about Frederick Douglass. I imagine Douglass would serve us all well right now for a bit of the everyday pain we may or may not feel. To move through it. To keep going.

Get around jails and halls of justice and the poetry of Whitman's house and these books, they are a refuge.

White people are roaming around downtown Camden. They have been described as zombies, because they tatter and they drag. The white people hanging out by the court are asking for money for something to eat or drink and they are met by a series of curt nos. The people of color from what I see aren't having it.

Most of the white people I see are mixing it up behind Walt Whitman's house. There is a large tree and where the houses are gone there is a field. Whitman's brother lived on this block; Whitman too. But that house is gone. There is music playing and people are partying. They are drinking and smoking so it is not loud, but the energy is frantic. It feels like the tail end of a family reunion. I never think to walk over and ask any of these folks about the Whitman House or what they think about anything. People is people, an old friend said. It is true. This party isn't mine though, so I just stand off to the side and watch some, because they've got the music going and so it feels like a park too.

Writing down here is to be set up to see a lot of people's gatherings dwarfed by the misery of these institutions. But, the Free Public Library, what can it mean here? I wonder, where are people supposed to go? To get some relief from the jail and the Hall of Justice? The laughs come and go together. The lawyers (the other white people besides the police) are talking about filing their papers. Papers. The law is reading and interpretation. The lawyers provide representation. Where would we be without our books? The public library is quiet for the free public. It is shut up.

The corrections officer laughed, and he told me that libraries are a thing of the past. A visible consignment to the past.

The New Jersey Transit River Line clangs its way through this area of downtown. I am told that Whitman liked the sound of the train, the Amboy Rail line that crossed just a block or so away from his home. He kind of liked to be in the mix.

On edge. People here. Dry-mouthed edge, gun-edge sharp, a circle of police at the Hall of Justice almost tipping over at the weight of their guns.

The police officers come on and off duty and seem to enjoy being outside together. They have ordered sausages from the sole food cart parked street side in front of the Hall of Justice. Just around the cart it smells very good, like grilled spiced meat. Four guys in a circle make easy conversation with the people moving all around them. But the officers are strapped with guns and this joins them at the hip.

Writing outside is suspect. Observing the outdoors or being inside oneself, or both. I notice that I'm not the only one musing on the small assembly of lunching policemen. Their presence here is a scaffold that telegraphs and ripples, like the surveillance tower located just a few blocks from here at the Walter Rand Transportation Center.

As I get up to leave, make my walk back to the PATCO station, another Puerto Rican observer calls to me.

It isn't that cold, Mami.

He's watched me bundle up in my new blue coat. I smile at him and he just says,

God bless you.

What tenderness abounds? I make my way until I find a ledge and perch at the bricks that wall up the Hall of Justice. A temporary writing desk for me. I set my notebook at my lap so I can write down a thought. All the surveillance cameras watch the block. To write in public. To be seen. To be open to the landscape and the visions of others too. A bit of beauty. A kind of offering. The lawyers and their papers, the battles of representation—to think about here—a public display of closure and literacy at the alcove of the Hall of Justice.

The jail organizes the block. Takes the place you have loved and turns it into a cage. Writing and reading publics. The people outside, together, using, gathered, the poetics of this landscape. Sidetracked here. Confrontation here between the being together disruption of the jail, so many! And the being together of poetry. Felled trees, greens. Grass and broken things remade into sitting chairs. Calling out to each other. The day care center, an old African American day care center is a good neighbor to the Whitman House, I am told. Always a good neighbor. Loved ones choosing to use with other people who are using. What that looks like from the outside is different from what that looks or feels like from within. You can't bring anyone back—not the poet, not them the living—but their spirit abounds. The forms of living and suffering, of life and desire, so much longing for feeling here, I think. That's a call. The jail calls out; people come to investigate, to use, right outside. Buy, sell, trade. There is so much here that agitates against being settled. Some kind of harmony here, too, at the uses of poetry, drugs, between one thousand jailed bodies and the streets calling, green calling, prison boulevard?

"This was the most exciting house in the world." In Eleanor Ray's recollections of playtime adventures with her siblings in the cellar of Walt Whitman's house, she notes that he died upstairs, "right in the bed." Eleanor's older brother Walter is the first to read the plaque on Walt Whitman's bed that signaled the object held some part of the poet's passing. Eleanor Ray and her family lived just next door; their house pressed right up next to Whitman's house. They'd watch as visitors streamed in and out of the house, and notice the changed faces of the visitors after their time in the house, the pleasure and the awe of being inside and among Whitman's haunt and things. For Eleanor Ray and her siblings there was "something alive in that house." Often it was them; they played there.

As an adult Eleanor Ray was appointed curator of the Walt Whitman House. In a published piece entitled "The Cellar," Eleanor describes the physical attributes of the cellar, the space below the Walt Whitman House, and a feeling of dread at a presence that abided there, that made its way or rejoined the general spirit of the house upstairs. African American children, four brothers and two sisters, she and her siblings played imaginatively through the dank, earthy, "suffocating atmosphere of the cellar." Eleanor Ray and her siblings flash light through the bottom of the house, attacking all fears and darkness, knowing as they did that they neighbored the most "exciting house in the world."

The children move between the upstairs and cellar and outdoors. Ray hones in on the bed that Whitman died in, his bed that still rests today in his upstairs bedroom. A plaque nailed at the footboard inscribes that he died here, in that very bed. The children check the veracity of that statement, Whitman's death in the bed, in the plaque, in the words of Mrs. Davis, the caretaker of the house at the time, who confirms it, and, too, in their own general feeling or sense of things. This authenticates Whitman's death, held here in the everyday object, a bed, that rests them each night, too, in the privacy of their own next-door household, and in the Whitman House's own underground, the cellar that runs the length of it all, where they sense the thinness of the border between the living and the dead. The cellar's proximity to both earth and house is raw and tomblike and generative of feeling. The children negotiate all this feeling and rawness and come up with a way of organized play that exacts a method to contend with the specificity of this terrain that seems on the precipice of scene, between the orders of life and death. Just how an ordinary bed can become a deathbed, and emptied of a body, can become an object of contemplation.

Eleanor Ray describes the system that she and her siblings worked out to investigate the Whitman House cellar and their work to remove the ashes from the furnace. Each sibling had a role and a placement in a line—Eleanor herself would be in the third position in the line, behind two of her brothers. She would watch for unusual movements and unusual sounds, and another brother would act as her second senses, "verifying" her "observations." The children subject their perceptions to each other and to their own system of play, work, and knowing. The remaining sister held open the door at the top of the staircase, while the youngest brother held open the back door off the cellar. The siblings assembled themselves to bring in a path to movement, in case they should need to flee in either direction: up or out. They attend to their own wonder, and it is always accompanied by a taste of fear and the bravery and forethought of their own wits and familial companionship. Six children clear and take out the ashes. Eleanor Ray lays down the story of her childhood work and care, the sense of place that the siblings enact in their play that makes the cellar possible, pleasurable, and memorable. She installs her childhood practices into the underground wonder and history of the Walt Whitman House.

As Eleanor Ray would do as an adult, as children she and her siblings scope out the daily visitors from around the world, from the comfort and position of their own porch. Outside, she sees the visitors come and go, and she notes their changed and charged expressions, their countenance after their encounters with the things and the wonder of the house, which she spirits in her play and in her recollection. Reflecting on what she and her siblings left there as children, traces of their play that avoided using the electricity and instead hinged on their own tactics and a flashlight, Eleanor Ray offers the play of Camden's own Black children as essential to the meaning she makes of the place. Indeed, the day the flashlight drops, and she finds herself stuck, enclosed in the cellar, she feels the cellar as a place of true dread. That dread is thick. She writes:

> We were always on guard. It was as though we expected something to happen. But, when it happened, we were hopelessly unprepared. Walter dropped the flashlight. It broke. There was no light. It was unbelievably dark. The cellar seemed like a tomb. All the dead in the world seemed to come alive. They sucked up all the air. And held it. I couldn't breathe. They were all around me. I couldn't move. Something cold and wet touched the back of my neck. I became tense, stiff all over. I even lost my voice. I tried to scream, but no sound came.

After what seemed like hours, I heard voices coming down the cellar steps. It was my brothers. They had brought Mrs. Davis to get me out of the cellar.[1]

When the flashlight goes their play is snuffed out. The collective of her brothers and sister vanishes in the darkness of the cellar and is replaced by an innumerable and overpowering "seeming," a dead that "sucks" and "holds" the air. In this atmosphere Eleanor Ray is surrounded, and her sense of movement and sound is taken, her voice and her scream. Her brothers recover her, and Mrs. Davis escorts Eleanor Ray up and out. It is a harrowing and truly sensory rendition of terror, perhaps not the assembly and touch of what "seems" to be the dead, but the loss of her voice, her breath and sound. Although she can hear—and indeed she registers the returning presence of her siblings through their approaching voices—Ray's only partial perception is, perhaps, part of how the dread works: the awareness of the loss of one's own expressive powers, made real in the world by scream and flight.

The dread follows Eleanor Ray into her adult work in the Walt Whitman House. She checks each room, searches out a feeling of a presence. Her childhood experiences and ideas accompany her into how she will move through the space, with memory and some vigilance. She writes: "The memory of that incident set strong on my mind, smothering the joy of being appointed curator of the Walt Whitman House in 1955, even though I knew I didn't have to contend with an unlighted cellar. The house had been totally restored by that time. It was the uncomfortable feeling that I wasn't alone in the house. The feeling was stronger in the rooms, which Whitman had used. He occupied the front parlor downstairs, and the front bedroom upstairs."[2]

The cellar and the house above, particularly the rooms in which Whitman lived, given his physical immobility, are places of spiritual potency, and the children and years later the woman guide, map potential flight. Eleanor Ray's treatment of her curatorship emerges from a sense of an inaugural tension between play and captivity, fear and wonder. What brings Eleanor Ray to wholeness in her own position in the house, as curator, and the house's benevolence is finally her commitment to the study of Whitman's writings. The readership that devotes itself to integration and visitation, Eleanor Ray at the Whitman body, archives, house. This stance repositions her in the house, allowing her to negotiate the space, the rooms where Whitman dwelled amongst his things, while carrying the haunting into and through its renovation and her tenure as guide.

The children who take out the ash, whose work is situated below, but who imbue their work with play and live next door, surround and make the house lively. "We kids" refuse to drag the electrical cord downstairs to light a way, and instead they count on their own assembly and a flashlight to see and navigate the space. In their decisions, skepticism, and hurry they surround Whitman. The ghost that is ever just a sense, a touch, appears in the memory of a childhood, and is then willed away at the text, the words and poems that cover Whitman's leftover things, so that his occupying spirit can depart. The poems do not constitute a haunting. They clear out the dead.

My own dream of the Whitman House had no Whitman, no dread, only the old lady. Years before I could go in for a visit, despite growing up not very far away, I dreamed that I was welcomed inside the house by Whitman's caregiver-maid. She brought me in and upstairs, and also into a ground-level room. I recall the light and the way my own liveliness cramped the space. When I awoke, and throughout the subsequent years, and perhaps always, this is what I gathered. I take it to mean, Go ahead, write! What I gather from Eleanor Ray is how to study to shake loose a fear. A fear of the dead. A haunting. How to wrap it in language in order to clear out enough room for the breath and force of life. A reading and a course of study that is necessary if we are to acknowledge the dead ones, and the place of it all, and make peace with it, not to evacuate, but to properly put in the work. This became the grounds for her to curate when the curator is a guide to movement. The architecture of the house folds in these people too.

From part four of Whitman's "I Sing the Body Electric":

> I have perceiv'd that to be with those I like is enough,
> To stop in company with the rest at evening is enough,
> To be surrounded by beautiful, curious, breathing, laughing flesh
>   is enough,
> To pass among them or touch any one, or rest my arm ever so
>   lightly round his or her neck for a moment, what is this
>   then?
> I do not ask any more delight, I swim in it as in a sea.

There is something in staying close to men and women and look-
      ing on them, and in the contact and odor of them, that
      pleases the soul well,
All things please the soul, but these please the soul well.[3]

There is the presentation of a childhood, of a time in Camden, the 1940s, when this mode of relation, play, joy, fear—the maneuvering of those things, gathered here at this site. When Ray begins to study the po- etry, her fear recedes. Her writing is sure to create a lively and bodily encounter between these times and practices, childhood and the dead, play and study. It is the breathless flight of children, ghosts in Camden. When she is asked years later whether Walt Whitman still abides in the house at 330 Mickle Boulevard, she says she knows where Whitman is—in Harleigh Cemetery.

George Hutchinson, in his "Afterword: At Whitman's Grave," de- scribes a meeting with Eleanor Ray.[4] He then heads out to Harleigh Ceme- tery. You can get lost looking for the grave, the mausoleum is tucked up under it all. Swampy; it floods in the rain. As someone who grew up off River Road and who has seen Camden floods, it is comforting that Walt Whitman abides here, too, in the wet green richness, the mix of it all. His body in Camden. Hutchinson climbs Whitman's tomb to look out.

That perspective and position, just above the house, at a window, or stuck inside, also strikes me as Camden, a vantage point for many. For the elder Whitman, when he was confined to a wheelchair and spent days at his window. To climb, to move the body in other ways, to adapt and move in tandem with place or one's (built) environment and to meet a barrier and hop, jump, or climb it, to see or be in space another way. Craft an- other movement to experience enjoyment.

The pain of this contracts, and then an acknowledgement and a rec- ognition. That we, too, are on the outside now and feel a longing and a sense of loss. A desire to go home. We share this from opposite sides of the shore.[5] Congregate life. Assembling in public, gang injunctions, Latino workers awaiting work, white folks partying behind Whitman's house, Black people too. All of us drive down the values. Blues life in the weather, in the world.

If demolition was and is an organized response to neighborhood life, then we suffered through it and still made a way for life in and around the shapes they left behind on the landscape: the square of an empty lot is maybe a place where people will always gather, a tree line free from the arrangement of row homes now opening up another view of the sky. Free fire zones.

Self and property. My recollections aren't enough to make me want to rebuy or purchase our house. Own it. Take it back. A friend says:

You should buy the house. I bet it'll be really cheap.

I pondered this for some time. It is said out of love and out of concern. My friends, too, have their memories there. To buy back the house. It isn't the broken walls or flooded basement that keeps me away. The excitement of a redesign, making improvements to the house: none of it makes any sense to me. When I was a girl the ceiling of the dining room had giant holes in it. When my dad got his VA settlement in 1986, after he was diagnosed 100 percent disabled from the war, we celebrated that yes, he was legitimately fucked up. My dad put $8,000 in cash—the number of dollars that corresponded to a payout for the years he suffered, that suffering a kind of free labor—into one of my mom's 1980s pocketbooks, a beige one that had a detachable strap, and he hid it up in the roof, accessible through the hole in the dining room ceiling. You'd have to stick your hand up through the hole and into the ceiling to feel it and pull it out. My mom's sewing machine used to sit there, just below the hole, and then later a single bed.

You would see holes in the walls as you made your way up the stairs. This used to embarrass me. Not our poverty, because everyone I knew was poor, all my friends were poor, too, but all the holes in the ceiling and the walls. The faded wallpaper and the crumbling sheetrock. Sometimes I'd sit at the stairs and touch the sheet rock. Pick at it like a scab while I talked to my middle school best friend, L, on the phone. The pull of the crumble, pull out a little piece and then try to set it back inside, a patchwork of bits. L was a dispatcher for her father's cab company, and if the line beeped through she'd have to put me on hold so she could answer it and dispatch a cab. Her dad's company was named Marco Cab—her father was Peruvian—and the company bore his name until the city of Camden made him rename it Supercab. When I'd call—and we talked almost every day, as best friends do—she'd answer the telephone, "Marco Cab." And then she'd hear my voice and we'd just get to talking about middle school things. My sisters and I used the stairwell to talk to our friends on the telephone. We'd pull the cord as far as it would go, reaching halfway up the stairs to give ourselves a bit of privacy.

It doesn't seem that buying back the house is what this is about. Or what we've come to. Or what I've come to understand. To hold a place here for us, it isn't happening in owning this home. Or having a piece of property here that we can go inside or pass down. It isn't in cultivating a garden. We've buried so much here. So many cats back there. That matters to me. The idea of owning this home and recovering something in that move, it causes me to feel something akin to returning to something that is no longer meant to be. To move into a kind of life that would be a mistake. That is, the draw and the care, the meaning, isn't in the access to the inside, to the walls, or to the feel of this house, to title and property, but in knowing that we've been opened up, that we are always going to be opened up to, surrender to, Camden. That we are part of the histories of this place, and that brings us back home, and histories and recollections exceed home, and the spirits in and of the things we've come through are there, yes, they are there for the taking.

What can't be handed down. No wealth there. See it all coming together as we are locked out. What keeps you from going in? You are not unwanted.

The geography of memory and a spatial imagination in Camden comprise some of these things. Objects and disintegration on a landscape reorganized by abandonment and disintegration. Rows upon rows of abandoned homes. And then one day only a single home is left standing across the street from your house. And you wonder at that happening there and then don't realize or know yet that it will cross the street. That you will be taken up by the same forces and all cast outside. And one day, too, your little house will be taken down. Boulevards and the softness of a windowed and wooden façade. The fullness of the stories, because we were at some kind of an ending, something that'd come to a catastrophic close. It could be a retreat. I know this now, a surrender. The loss and resignation of moving out or a kind of moving on. We can no longer do this here. We're leaving. It isn't a crashing down, but the coming to an understanding, a decision. Puerto Rican exhaustion.

The joy and tenderness of being home, hello to the house. Hello casa! The draw and "welcome home girls" of an old friend. We were here together. It mattered; it is in the house. We had a life. We had and kept secrets, made our privacies, and they are shut up in there.

Once I saw a bannister breathe. The wood expand, extend, and return to its usable shape. I heard a doorbell ring at night. Stairwells have come to me and floors have given up their positions and pattern and lifted up like small hills. The girls have come home for a visit. Come home. They've rerouted the 419 bus so that it will stop for you just in front of your house. All you have to do is cross the street. It is afternoon. The sun is out. You've come home from Ricardo's Pizza, after you've shared a cheese pizza, French fries, and a delicious cheesesteak.

My sister will venture into the backyard. I don't say this is excruciating but instead wonder at her ability to move in and through. I cannot bring myself to touch the house. My nieces play on the porch. The oldest has been inside, when my parents—her grandparents—and their cats and dogs were in there. Dad played music or watched TV. The little one talks to herself, turns an inward dialogue, her chin at chest, hands at hips, while her older sister swings at the rails and peers at the sky through a pair of new blue eyeglasses. The house is still ours right now. They make it that way. You could not tell me to go, but I can't bring myself to touch it, sit down at the porch, go in back, accompany my sister to see the view upstairs from the backyard. Maybe I have too many dreams, things that wake me up, sometimes with great comfort and insight, sometimes just disturbed, and that is what is in my way.

Listen, this isn't an exchange of ownership. No signs were hung, no open houses held. No new people making life and memories inside. Your house is coming to ruin. There is something in this process. We may not be the last ones, because people come to vacants—they might mostly come to hide—but we are the last ones when it was marked as owned, legitimate private property. Being forced out may sever something in that arrangement. It may be part of securing an even more forceful blow, that this is how it begins, how capital renews itself.

Mr. H sees us standing about outside. He comes our way with warm greetings, and we talk. He's invited us back to his house for lunch tomorrow, but I'm headed out of town. My mother lent his wife a cake pan once. It was blackened with years of use, but it was one of her good ones. When his wife returned the pan to my mother it was silver again. She had used some type of cleaning agent, some elbow grease, exercised some time getting my mother's pan super clean. It looked new. When she returned the pan, it was like receiving this whole other brand-new pan. My mother laughs a good-natured astonishment. She says:

Chica! Wow!

We all laugh. And I can hear in my mother's voice a return to the joys of talking to a girlfriend. My mother did all the housework and she did it every single day, all the cooking, too, but seeing how our neighbor got this pan to look like that, that took us all someplace. Told us something about ourselves, and then, too, the spirit of care and consideration in the person who walked that pan back across the street.

Because our parents are gone now, moved away, we use the pen Mr. H carries in his shirt pocket to write my mom's new cellphone number on a box of Popeyes chicken, some of what's left of his lunch, so he can get in touch with them if he wants to.

My sister works at a nonprofit for a time. Our mother worked there, too, for a time, in the 1980s, helping my grandmother prepare food at a halfway house. Halfway to freedom or halfway from incarceration? Halfway to a house? Anyway, I remember going there as a child, into the kitchen where my grandmother prepared food. My grandmother is talented and a maker. She worked many jobs simultaneously to make ends meet. My oldest sister has inherited these gifts. I recall that the kitchen of the halfway house had very large cans of food stuff and coffee. Everything was proportioned as if for Alice in Wonderland. My grandmother worked the food and my mother helped her out I suppose. My mother has a hard time remembering this; she laughs off her forgetting. Maybe it is stress and sleeplessness, but Alzheimer's got her dad and his mom in a way, so maybe it is coming down the line for us too. Turning Camden through us and through our memories is some lovely part of remembered life. Keeping the beauty of it all with us every time we read.

When my sister works for the nonprofit she tells me that she looks at pictures of current clients who are residents. Some will come to occupy different houses. For each house they occupy there is a corresponding picture, a portrait of their face. She flips through (clicks through) the photos and the residents change and age before her eyes. She says that of all she has experienced here, this is what moves her the most. Watching folks change, their hairstyles and colors, their skin, the way they look out, smile. Between seven and fifteen years a person moves into and out of different halfway houses and after being incarcerated for a time. You can wonder after a life's experiences: an open face, hard lines around her eyes and mouth. Vulnerable at this stage of life, made to come before the camera again as a document of her experiences with these systems and forms of help and habitation.

My sister tells me she was driving in Camden on her way to her long-time eye doctor and the feeling of being back home began to come to her.

This ride is the bumpy one down 27th Street. When we were kids, the church van would slow at the potholes in patchwork streets and, depending who was driving and their speed, you would fly up a bit in your seat. Row homes on opposite sides of the narrow street were variously barred at windows, porches, some with small fences that demarcated the privacy of a front yard. The traffic on this street was regular and residents hung outside and interacted, cooled off on porches, watched the cars stream by. One house sold ice cream, Puerto Rican–style limber; a homemade cardboard sign in their window read: "We do limber."

These sights bring my sister back to another feeling. It is distinct from the place where she now resides, the home she keeps with her kids and her family. She has another creative sound in her voice when she is talking about being in Camden and feeling like she was going home. When I have had the chance to witness my mom in Puerto Rico, I see her and hear her there so differently too. She is happier, a kind of before time, when none of us were in her life, and she was connected to this place. I like that this connection is so powerfully present there, that it makes its way into the sounds of her voice. A girlhood emerges there. It is a girlhood that is rooted and that makes itself known, at least to me.

My sister is browsing the internet at work and discovers that our Camden house has sold. Sold for something like $17,000. But when she looks back for the page, to see it again, she cannot find it anymore. It appears that she has lost the page.

She says she will drive by again. Drive by the house again. To say goodbye. She lives not so far away; a drive is possible. She can make the trip. She continues talking to me about this, but I have stopped listening to her. It is not out of disinterest or malice. I feel my sister is gliding over rough waters. She's moving with an ease or competence. I wonder, are these her waters or my own? The waters are neck high and you are unsure of the shoreline and you freak out a bit inside, but do not betray this on the outside, because it doesn't go with what looks like the ease of her strokes and I do not want to upset her or seem like I am no longer able to listen. I am no longer able to listen.

When I was a girl I woke up with sore hands, like I had been working all night on an assembly line, or with tiny scratches next to my nose or under my eye. I remember telling my mother my hands hurt and her concern, but then waking up once and finally realizing that I slept tight fisted. That I was doing it to myself.

That night a series of dreams: We are all together at the house. My dad, my sisters, my mom. There is so much light! There is a general feeling of goodwill among us. I sit at the bottom of the staircase, where the dining room meets the way to the upstairs. I am at the landing, seated on the floor. Looking up I feel the fullness of our lives here. There is no pain. This bears repetition. I see layers of wallpaper. Each piece is different, and I see decades in the designs and motifs represented on the papers. They are ornate, whimsical, geometric; I see the happy forms of shapes and I wonder after the work of generations. Overlapping, broken, lost, dispossessed. But this does not bring me sadness, only encounters and the light of a day and being with these people in the room, people who would allow you your inward life, who would not say get up, stop thinking, stop feeling what you are feeling. Here I can see the dreams of some Puerto Ricans. Just here. I take this all as a small revelatory gift. There is a hand at the shoulder, a comradery and a course that says we were in celebration of a beauty, our own. And it lingers at these walls, at the landing, in memory and the flights of sleep and wrestling with what you may have initially thought of as sad.

There is a sense of shock and then a stupidity, a kind of, of course. That feeling is on course with what it has meant to be a Puerto Rican, a Puerto Rican in Camden.

I ship Dad CBD products, oils to alleviate the pain. He's suffering through prescriptions of oxy. Eighty milligrams a day, which is making him so constipated. That Dad is one of the many people taking opioids, one of many Vietnam-era veterans, is a strange comfort. An understanding of a shared pain. That his own father succumbed to "addiction" puts this into another kind of context for me. I want so much for my father to be free. I want my grandfather back. I want to know what it feels like to have a father and a grandfather who aren't overcome by suffering. Of course, that is ridiculous. The way Dad and his dad have suffered is human. It is ethical to feel pain, to not be able to get over it, to prop it on your head like a jeweled thing.

When the house was lost to us I was in a state of stupid shock. I've decided to hold the house as a witnessing place. A go-to sanctuary, relief from the day place. Losing the house, watching it go, come to ruin, I realize we were always in it. That the processes at work on the neighborhood around us, that we were part of, were coming for us too. Why wouldn't we come out the same way? How would we be any different or spared? I saw the houses demolished one by one. We were the girls. We were the young women. I saw the boys and the young men disappear. This was not natural, but it was time. Another time. Then it came to us too. And were swept up in it too. My dad was lit up the last time I saw him at the house.

Dad had gone first. But he'd returned. He got on the sofa and his eyes were lightning sharp. I saw Dad and his psychosis felt like a weapon, only turned on me. For the first time I felt like a stranger in my home. The whole house felt different, but this wasn't fear of mental illness, if that's what it is called. I've been lit myself. This was whatever Dad had to work out and it was bigger than us and it ran through the house, maybe just that one day.

What does it mean to get right up next to it, to explore, to make them new or different, make them a part of the matter of this place? Well, for me, it is a source of humility and a constant reminder to critical thinking that we were never meant to be reduced to numbers, to the subject, object of study; or it means we have to accompany our stories, to draw each other out, in kindness and in a greater understanding. We are not to starve or be dispossessed. When that has been the bulk of what it has meant to be Puerto Rican and Black in this place. The arrogance of our erasures. That Camden is suitable for poetry. See Whitman. See Rasheeda. See J. At the waterfront in the seventeenth-century, captured Africans were made ready for slavery. After waters, after ocean and total loss, Camden was the threshold of oblivion, the edge of violence.

Before heading back to meet my sister, I walk around the transportation center, exploring some of the local shops. As kids we'd come down here and visit the doctor's office and, we'd hope, stop at McDonald's before catching the bus home. My mom might take us if she had enough money to buy us all food. It'd be a nice remedy for whatever shots we'd gotten, but mostly for the long wait we'd endured at the clinic. Same-day appointments or not, my mother brought us to a clinic that filled my small heart with something like resentment. I could not name why, but it lay in the tone and looks my mother received and my mother's refusal to give it back. What was it my mother possessed? Maybe being born elsewhere. Maybe a combination of that and faith and her own general kindness: then, she treated people all the same. We might wait two hours for the doctor, then wait some more in the examination room. We never had anything super wrong with us; the visits were mostly checkups. They tested my patience, those waits, in faded plastic bucket seats, surrounded by colorful drab and posters reminding parents to keep an eye out for lead paint in three or four different languages. I resented the posters, because they were yellowing and depressing and I concentrated my vision at those two kids drawn into their image, a brother and sister playing next to a radiator and contemplating their own faded and chipped walls.

McDonald's was a joy to me then, before my mother assembled us at the corner, exact change in hand for the short bus ride home to Cramer Hill. These bus waits were another test, all the ways that being together, moving together in poverty can suck the joy out of childhood or make something else come through. I suppose being sick as a kid and having to wait for a bus in both directions can feel like some kind of misery.

At a hip-hop–inflected clothing store, I purchase two pairs of socks, colorful Tribe Called Quest *Midnight Marauders* socks and a black-and-white pair, with Jackie Robinson poised at bat. I'd asked after any type of Camden gear, so that I could bring back a present for my son and his father, but they have nothing here like that. The girls working at the register think together about where I could go to get some Camden gear, but they can't think of anything just downtown, so I settle on the socks. I remember waiting for the River Line one day some years before, headed to Trenton and then New York, and it was a sunny day and a little farmer's market was happening. Someone was playing Bob Marley, and this filled me with a special kind of happiness, hearing his voice, its textures turning through the Camden skies. That music. Holding the socks, I think about their message of being here in Camden, for me. The absence just now of Camden gear, but being able to see my boyfriend walking around our house in these socks and remembering a day when I was home and I shopped and it felt really normal, and when the shop owner paused his long cellphone conversation to greet me I told him it would be great to get some Camden gear up in here. Shops that sell clothing were a rarity for a time, maybe even still.

When we went downtown during the Christmas holiday my mother would go to Wilmar Christian Bookstore. They sold Bibles and Christian living books, and also tables of knickknacks and figurines. The gift part of the bookstore. The tables and shelves that lined the small, dark shop had ample room. I'd read the short messages engraved on clocks and other small devices that could be made to sing for the Lord in addition to performing their function. I imagine my mother purchased our bibles here, engraving some with our names. My oldest sister received a bible that was held in a soft leather binding. They put her name on the front. It was lovely. When they decided to get me a bible some years later—I guess I was ready—I asked for one like my sister's. The softness and the give, this was a quality of holding her book, but when my book arrived it was pebbled and rigid. My name was on it though, and my sister filled in the "on this day" information in her lovely script. So somehow her voice and hand are in there still, if not in the feel and shape of the book.

My dad's bible was red, and it had the Jesus words printed in red. It was all in Spanish. My mom ended up using it because Dad never did and eventually he gave it to her. She wore it out. So much study. My bible is still like new, except that it has split down the spine. My father seemed to prefer science fiction, and for a time he'd take us to the Cherry Hill Mall with him on Saturdays when his car ran. We'd follow him into the bookstore and then up to the register as he purchased two or three paperbacks. He'd disappear upstairs for the next two to three days. He'd emerge when he was done reading the books. Dad got lost in the reading experiences. We were jealous; we wanted our own books and barbies, but the same time it kept Dad interesting and also freed us up to be fatherless for a few days, freed us up from the pressures of his sadness and well-attended grief.

Besides Wilmar, I was fascinated by the display in Elsie's Botanica, a gift shop then located at Federal Street, just in front of the 404 bus stop where we'd wait for the bus to the mall, where I'd be dropped off every day in July when I was older and participated in PRIME (Philadelphia Region Introducing Minorities to Engineering) in Philadelphia. The lives of the saints; Lazarus a hobbled man whose cuts were attended to by dogs, their lick and saliva. All of this thrilled me. My younger sister stopped in most days to get a soda for her walk home from middle school, when desegregation sent her to East Camden Middle School instead of Vets. In Elsie's she got a close look at the figures and Santeria stuff and perhaps it nourished her own appreciation of the macabre.

My sister and I sit on our father's bed during one of his frequent naps. He tries to explain to us that he is hurting. He says that it is as if there is a crack at the back of his skull, an invisible fault line that runs down the back of his head. The hurt comes from there. We inspect the back of his head, but we see only his dark, coarse, unruly hair, my sister's inheritance. From then on I look at our dad differently. I imagine a wounding unseen, and at such an unfortunate spot, on the head. We were shipwrecked with our father, the two of us, on a sunny afternoon in Camden. What could we do to improve his lot? To unmake the pain, the scar we could not even see. The scar that was, in fact, not real?

A line of abandoned and vacant homes laced our vision, the farthest we could see, then. I keep calm, break off, pushed so far back from my surroundings, vigilant mode, watching, writing to gain back the distance, pull it all close, again?

The house is set back some from the sidewalk. The boards are up. Nothing indicates that it has been sold. A paper plate is stuck in the window. What used to be or function as the window, indicated by the shape. Something is written on the paper plate. I can't tell. Things are taking on newness in their shape, new functions. Wood to glass to paper.

It has been a troubled writing. Getting to it. Maybe that is the point too. But it contains some of what has mattered most to me. Being together. Being there without the threat of being killed or mistaken for refuse, the people who don't matter or are merely matter. It shouldn't be this way, but it disturbs me, even still.

Next door a fence creates a gathering place for the church. The church covers a small set of stairs with a large ramp. They erect a canopy that covers its length and install fluorescent lights to guide worshippers up and in. Dad attended but then got turned off. He stops going, says, if I recall, that they are too close-minded around sexualities and the spirit. But then again, this is only what they say. They cannot all be the same, of one mind. But it is the message and so he closes the blinds and acts cool yet distant to that community of his once fellow worshippers. He nods, whistles, and smiles his way right into the house when they are in session, in service.

The last time I am in the house is when it is furnished (a revisit). I am with my daughter and son and boyfriend. My dad barely looks at me. He's on fire in his mind. I can tell. Dishes are scattered all over the floor, random cups from eating day and night. I'll say the place feels different, a new phase, so perhaps I hold onto the cups because they are a mainstay. A Cuban neighbor is over to the house too. He is one of the members of a family that Dad takes under his wing. Dad takes out a loan and gives them a bunch of money so the brothers can buy a used car and we all object, we are protective of Dad (too much) and suspicious of the newbie neighbors. But we are wrong. They pay him back slowly and completely from their salaries from Walmart. They use the car to get to work. I buy Mom a TV for the upstairs bedroom because Dad hogs the downstairs, but Dad gives it to the Cubans a few months later. Mom waves it off when I object. It really pisses me off until I wave it off too. It is just stuff. What is the real point?

I go upstairs to use the bathroom and the house is still away from me. I can't nail it. A new vibe, a new phase. I pee on what is floating in the toilet and wonder after my father's new life.

When Mom leaves the house, Dad objects. He bags up all her stuff, gets help doing it too. And he leaves it in trash bags on the porch. A mad cruelty. Mom had to go. My sisters agreed. She feels unsafe. Dad has gone a few times, too, himself. Mom loses many things. People take the bags from the front porch! Eventually she returns to the house and then Dad leaves. He cannot take it anymore, he says. Maybe not Mom, not her, but the presence of the church pressing up against the house? Boxed in and wondering about what illuminates you and can bring you to closeness with God? Dad is paranoid that he is being talked about in the neighborhood, in the church, so he takes off. He says it is the Camden wreckage, but I imagine it is the pressure of wanting out.

The last time I am inside, before the pipes are stolen and the water bursts and the boards cover the windows—such a lovely little house. Empty of us and our stuff, our love, our cruelties, and our awkward dreaming. That's when I unscrew a hook from the back of our bedroom door and take it with me.

My sister tells me in conversation that she is having a harder time reckoning with the house sold—that another family or people will live there now. She expected it to go to ruin. I did too. We didn't think it would be sold as is and then restored bit by bit by a Vietnamese man on a ladder. When we talk about it I listen and wonder about her shifts, about the range of feelings and reckonings that she, too, must contend with. There is sadness there. Once she appreciated the beauty of a ruin, the lifetimes that are there perhaps, or the colors and textures of it. Perhaps she still does. I do too. This was the landscape of our imagination, not some wondering about a particular past, not very much, but a being in the present, held together there, in and by, holding it together too.

She had lived here with her first daughter, in our upstairs bedroom. So much of her life here. As I listen I wrestle back my own unease, the parts of me that shut down all talk of this, because it feels bigger than spoken words, because for me it is all written so that I might give it a form, a space, a direction, a reading. And then decide it is not enough. We listen and talk to each other about Camden. About other Camden folk who have passed on and who were loved and how to grieve them and the ongoing conditions that make their deaths statistical.

For me, the idea of that house, our house, being a house for people, for a Vietnamese family, if the new owner holds onto it, keeps it for his own people or rents it to others. I find comfort there now. That other people will be housed here too, that they will live abundantly here, it brings me happiness that day and today. We didn't profit in a sale. We can attend to our lives, our memories, and our being in place; we can say goodbye and return many times, always. For me this understanding, this meaning, isn't quantifiable or exchangeable, but it is a set of relations worth passing on.

EPILOGUE

/

A small, windowless cement structure at the back of a fenced empty lot. The lot is property. It belongs to the church around the corner. The church occupies what was once, long before we arrived, a place called the Rio Theatre, a movie theatre. (What a joy for the lucky residents to have had a movie theatre here, within walking distance, just around the block.) The church must have been worried, because they got a couple of pit bulls to guard the structure and kept them inside it. Whatever is inside there to be guarded? No one comes to check on the dogs or to feed them or take them outside. They are forgotten. Their presence is finally revealed when someone eventually remembers them and comes. But it is too late. One of the pit bulls has killed and eaten the other one. They must have fought because they were starving. The victor doesn't last long and dies soon after. Waterless days, I imagine. When the church remembers they pull out one dead dog and he or she is just skin and bones, the giant imbalance of a skull. Dad tells me about this. He witnesses it, sees the dog carcass get pulled out, and then he is hit by a crash of flashbacks, the knives and nausea and heat of his Vietnam War experiences come back at him, and thirtysomething years collapse. He sweats it out at night, all the rage and the sadness turning in time here, across a slim street in our neighborhood, the monstrosity of an imbalanced skull and the disgust of the cement doghouse.

One day Mom looks out the window of our house and sees a group of young neighborhood guys with a pit bull that they are trying to set onto a kitten. Mom tears out of the house and yells at them: "What do you think you are doing? That's my cat!"

It isn't her cat though. Mom lies and claims the stray. The guys back off the kitten and mom scoops it up to add to her collection. It is tiny and has lost its mother too young and so Dad feeds it milk from a baby bottle that is left over from one of the granddaughters. The kitten grows up this way, nurtured and sleeping with Dad, coming to him when he calls, and we joke that this cat thinks of itself as a dog. When the kitten gets older their relationship begins to change, takes on the cool independence of most human–cat relations (as we've known them), and it amuses and comforts us that this cat loves Dad so much. He follows Dad around. Sits with him in the Lazy Boy. When the cat dies, some few years after Dad leaves Camden behind and takes an apartment in a complex suburb, he'll keep the cat's ashes on the windowsill, in a small wooden box embossed with his name. Dad will say that the cat, which had begun to come and go, exploring a new territory, had been poisoned. He will understand the cat's death as intentional, proof that nowhere is really safe, and that he himself, as a Puerto Rican, is unwelcome in this new neighborhood. We'll suck our teeth some at his paranoia, but really, it is probably true.

Listen, I could tell you that this project started with a kitten, a gift from my father. My calico cat. That the night someone shot a gun into our window to shut her up (she was in heat) I became a certain kind of writer. There. You might see folks holding their cat in a lap or pulling the covers up so that she can crawl between the crook in your legs each night to go to sleep. It was like that. I stepped into a language and thought to get something out of the experience of her death. The way it shook me to get up at a gunshot, a pop, and see her there, on the wooden floor below a window opened to the summer heat, with a destroyed head.

One August day my sisters and I open our parent's bedroom window and crawl out onto the little roof that overhangs the kitchen. We lay four bath towels onto the black tar roof. The towels are thin and short or thick and short, depending on how long they have been in our possession, how many washes they've endured. Made for bathrooms, not beaches or roofs. We sunbathe and give ourselves over to the roof as we are hidden from the North 27th Street view and all the people who come and go in their cars and on foot. We are exposed only to the sky and whatever flies overhead. If we prop ourselves up we can see the elementary school where our mom works and where we studied, too, empty now because it is the summertime. Still, we are careful to stay low. When I return to college a couple of weeks later, one of my professors asks me where I've been off to, because my skin is a holiday. The tender privacy of a tree that is just a weed, that we call the weed tree, but that gives us a partial shade and allows us a gentle look up to the air, to the sun. We are in a kind of paradise together here, having discovered the privacy of a backyard and a slight tar roof that is just wide enough to bear our collective weight. We crawl in and out of the window to retrieve our things, a glass of water, a bandanna, a book. Mom is just below us, sheltered in the kitchen. These are still the years my mother would hum and sing and fill our kitchen with a medley of Spanish tunes. She is probably standing up, reading a newspaper or something she's cut out from a magazine and will stash in her collection of clippings. She doesn't mind us or the towels we've pulled out, that we'll leave for her to wash, whether they will stain or whether the decades of dirt and rooftop detritus that will collect in our towels will transfer into the entire ropa sucia. Next door the German Maennerchor, now a Latino church, is quiet except for the hum of the air conditioner stuck in a window. The loudspeaker that they have installed to broadcast their services to the street is silent. The women who pray or sing at the pulpit microphone are from all across Central America. They grieve their homelands and they turn it into song and holy stuff. They don't boom like the men do; they are a current that travels another less annoying frequency, at least to me. Years later, my younger sister wages an imaginary war with the congregation when she is trying to get her baby to nap and her bedroom walls vibrate from the voices of the Sunday worshippers, who have sidestepped traditional outdoor services and door-knock witnessing, and instead rely on a speaker that allows them to broadcast full blast to the neighborhood while enjoying the shaded and air conditioned comfort of their makeshift sanctuary. Come back to the Lord. Come and be saved. But all in Spanish.

I wrote here in winter, at a wooden picnic table, adjacent to a few trees that had been planted to secure a view. The table might seat courthouse visitors or daily workers. They won't be run off. The picnic table will conjure and transport a season. This may not be the function of a midday lunch break, work on each side, but a picnic table is some part of the illusion. Just a few blocks away folks are tableless but perch on stumps and are living it up outside. I circle around the block and slow at a stone fence. I'd lost my writing place. What I could imagine here, the way I imagined here. I wonder, how long will Camden last? I settle into snow, into roof, into a curbside after the firemen have washed the man's blood away. Where does it go? It belongs here now, called to stay and be loved in small houses erected and party lamentations. Whatever drink is your choice. Put the empty bottle down here, the cup. I cannot remember what season it was. There was no snow on the ground.

My father climbs the Benjamin Franklin Bridge at night, when walking is forbidden, and the pedestrian walkway is closed. He climbs and hops the barricade. He tells us afterward. He goes into Philadelphia, corners and lots, itinerant preaching. He orders tomes of Christian theology over the telephone—three or four oversized and expensive books. We are poor and the books strike me with jealousy as beautiful and ridiculous. He probably spends $300 on the set. In a standoff with the police in two-thousand-and-something, Dad is talked down from a knife, from self-harm. Weeks later he is made to appear before a judge in a New Jersey courtroom about the incident. He tells the judge his story, about his experiences and his ideas, about Vietnam. He crafts a narrative and the judge and the court dismiss all charges and thank him for his service to his country. Afterward, we kind of get a kick out of his storytelling abilities, but really I am just relieved, then, as today. That the cops who showed up to answer a call did not shoot Dad. Just the other day in the place where I live now I heard three gunshots. They were so loud because they were around the block. They made landfall in a man who had been in the middle of the street and then tucked between two houses, in an alley, distressed. The police were called to help him, but they killed him. They said he had a gun. I heard the shots that killed the man. It dragged me back a few years and through several experiences, all at once. Gunshot a suspension and a dragging through time, out of time. It was just around the corner. We were changing the clocks that night, to save light. I mapped the kids in the house, told my daughter to move away from the window, to sit deeper in the house.

/

Prologue

1. According to local newspaper reports, the hospital public relations director and administrator "refused to release information regarding Jimenez's injuries, issuing only status reports." It was also reported that "information was being withheld from the public, the press and from the police upon the advice of both the hospital's and Jimenez's attorneys." "He (Jimenez) is apparently suffering from internal poisoning which allegedly resulted from the rupture of a diseased internal organ, which in turn was allegedly caused by a body trauma and/or strain immediately prior to his admission to the hospital on July 31, 1971." "Jimenez Reported to Be 'in a Coma,'" *Courier Post*, August 20, 1971, 29.

2. Lucas K. Murray, "Days of Rage: Summer Riots of 1971 Sparked Camden's Undoing," *Courier-Post*, August 21, 2011. In 1971 there were "about 16,000 Puerto Ricans, 35,000 blacks and about 50,000 whites living in this city across the Delaware River from Philadelphia. The Puerto Rican population has nearly doubled in the last 10 years, and currently there are no elected Puerto Rican officials."

3. Rebellion at Attica Prison in New York erupts September 13, 1971; imprisoned intellectual and Soledad Brother activist George Jackson is killed August 21, 1971, in San Quentin, California, just a day after Puerto Ricans set off rebellion in Camden.

4. Rick Barot, "Tarp," *Poetry Magazine*, May 2013, https://www.poetry foundation.org/poetrymagazine/poems/56241/tarp.

5. Lisa Stevenson, *Life Beside Itself: Imagining Care in the Canadian Arctic* (Oakland: University of California Press, 2014); Dean Spade, *Normal Life: Administrative Violence, Critical Trans Politics, and the Limits of Law* (Durham, NC: Duke University Press, 2015). Darnell Moore's beautiful memoir, *No Ashes in the Fire: Coming of Age Black and Free in America* (New York: Nation Books, 2018), opens with and treats these histories as well, thinking critically about Black Lives Matter and Camden's insurgent histories.

6. As today, the names of the victims of police brutality come to stand in for the scene of violence—and the newspapers I read from this time refer to the murder of Rafael Rodriguez/Horacio Jimenez as the "Jimenez Incident."

7. This excerpt is from a longer statement issued by William Yeager, Director of Public Safety. "Officials, Leaders in Opposite Stand on Rioting in City," *Courier Post*, August 20, 1971, 29.

8. Howard Gillette Jr., *Camden after the Fall: Decline and Renewal in a Post-Industrial City* (Philadelphia: University of Pennsylvania Press, 2005). Charles Poppy Sharp, chairman of the Black People's Unity Movement, is quoted expressing solidarity between Camden's communities of color: "We support the Puerto Rican community because we too have been victims of police brutality."

9. Joseph Bulser, "The Protestors," *Courier Post*, August 20, 1971.

10. Denise Ferreira da Silva, "No-Bodies: Law, Raciality and Violence," *Meritum (Belo Horizonte)* 9, no. 1 (2014): 119–62.

11. "20 Hurt, 40 Arrested as Rioting Hits Camden," *Courier Post*, August 20, 1971, 8.

12. Kevin Riordan, "Whitman House Caretaker Shares Legacy of City's Good Gray Poet," *Courier Post*, April 18, 1983.

13. "Broom Protected Whitman House," *Asbury Park Press*, December 26, 1971, A15; *Philadelphia Inquirer*, January 3, 1972.

14. Steve Klinger, "A Shrine to Whitman, But Too Few Know It," *Courier Post*, July 30, 1966.

15. Horace Traubel, August 23, 1891, in *With Walt Whitman in Camden*, vol. 8 (1996), 435. From the Walt Whitman Archive, https://whitmanarchive.org/criticism/disciples/traubel/WWWiC/8/whole.html.

16. Traubel notes of Whitman: "It is astonishing how little disposed he is to really throw his window open to the winds—will only open one of three windows. Yet I have repeatedly argued with him, and Longaker has done so with much emphasis. Now, today, he complained of heat. Yet, while hot out-of-doors a free breeze was blowing. Nights, again, he will close the door to Warrie's room, lock the hall door, and close the blinds of the shutter of one

window" (Saturday, August 22, 1891). In *With Walt Whitman in Camden*, vol. 8 (1996), 433. From the Walt Whitman Archive, https://whitmanarchive.org /criticism/disciples/traubel/WWWiC/8/med.00008.193.html.

17. In an autobiographical sketch, Whitman wrote: "As he recuperated and still found himself alive, in Camden some years ago he came across a little wooden cottage for sale; and having nearly the money required for it, he bought it (he was aided by G. W. Childs) and has lived in it ever since and lives there now. His special apartment or living and writing and sleeping place (has been likened to some big old cabin for a kinky sailor-captain of a ship) is a large room on the second floor front 20 by 22 feet in area with a couple of tables (one rough old mahogany one, a Whitman heirloom over 100 years old, and another made for him in Brooklyn by the poet's father), a stove, chairs, a good bed, several heavy boxes, and a big ample rattan-seated chair with timber-like legs, rockers and arms large as ship's spars with a huge wolf-skin spread over the back in winter, a plain but very comfortable and ponderous edifice-built retreat in which WW ensconces the greater part of his days and whence, using a tablet on his lap, he issues all his poems, essays and letters of late years. He has within reach a Bible (English ed'n), Homer, Shakspere [*sic*], Walter Scott's Border Minstrelsy, Prof. Felton's Greece, Macmillan's ed'n of Burns, and Longfellow's Dante with the old few other volumes he still reads lingeringly and never tires of. All around where he sits spreads a great litter of newspapers, magazines, letters, MSS, proofs, memoranda, slips, on chairs, on the floor etc., with pen and ink handy, and one or two bunches of flowers. As he cannot walk, hardly move or get up without assistance, he has abandoned any attempt at apparent order and what strict housekeepers would call neatness but lets his books and papers 'lay loose.' The only point he is particular about is careful ventilation." Quoted in Traubel, July 30, 1891, in *With Walt Whitman in Camden*, vol. 8 (1996), 375–76. From the Walt Whitman Archive, https://whitmanarchive.org/criticism /disciples/traubel/WWWiC/8/med.00008.170.html.

18. Traubel recounts a talk with Whitman: "Spoke of the beauty of the day. 'What did you do yesterday?' And I told him of our walk yesterday along Carsham Creek to Devil's Pool—Reeder, Longaker, Gilbert, Anne, along. He asked, 'Did Anne walk it? Six or seven miles? Good girl! It is a great thing to hear of the girls walking. She must be quite a walker.' And further, 'How well I know what such walks mean! What they lead to.' I happened to say *Leaves of Grass*. 'How well I know what *that* leads to. Its value is not in what it exhibits but in what it stirs us to exhibit—not in what it brings but what it leads us to find ourselves.' And he exclaimed, 'Good! Good! I hope it is! That is what we have always had before us—that is the sort out of which all the rest comes—a few indicative splashes—a little field—trail—then

silence.'" Sunday, July 5, 1891, in *With Walt Whitman in Camden*, vol. 8 (1996), 302. From the Walt Whitman Archive, https://whitmanarchive.org/criticism/disciples/traubel/WWWiC/8/med.00008.145.html.

19. Quoted by Traubel, Tuesday, September 15, 1891, in *With Walt Whitman in Camden*, vol. 8 (1996), 510. From the Walt Whitman Archive, https://whitmanarchive.org/criticism/disciples/traubel/WWWiC/8/med.00008.217.html.

20. Traubel, Tuesday, September 22, 1891, in *With Walt Whitman in Camden*, vol. 8 (1996), 544. From the Walt Whitman Archive, https://whitmanarchive.org/criticism/disciples/traubel/WWWiC/8/med.00008.224.html.

21. Traubel, August 25, 1891, in *With Walt Whitman in Camden*, vol. 8 (1996), 438. From the Walt Whitman Archive, https://whitmanarchive.org/criticism/disciples/traubel/WWWiC/8/med.00008.196.html.

22. James Baldwin wrote: "In our image of the Negro breathes the past we deny, not dead but living yet and powerful, the beast in our jungle of statistics. It is this which defeats us, which continues to defeat us, which lends to interracial cocktail parties their rattling, genteel, nervously smiling air: in any drawing room at such a gathering the beast may spring, filling the air with flying things and an unenlightened wailing. Wherever the problem touches there is confusion, there is danger. Wherever the Negro face appears a tension is created, the tension of a silence filled with things unutterable. It is a sentimental error, therefore, to believe that the past is dead; it means nothing to say that it is all forgotten, that the Negro himself has forgotten it. It is not a question of memory. Oedipus did not remember the thongs that bound his feet; nevertheless the marks they left testified to that doom toward which his feet were leading him." James Baldwin, *Notes of a Native Son* (Boston: Beacon Press, 2012), 29–30.

23. "Francisco Rodriguez, Rafael's father, filed suit in August 1972, seeking $250,000 in damages and alleging negligence on the part of the patrolmen and the city. Out-of-court negotiations resulted in an offer of $5,000 from the city and $10,000 from the Insurance Company of North America." The article continues: "At least half of the $15,000 settlement will reportedly go to pay remaining hospital and funeral bills and Medicaid payments stemming from the death." Larry Reibstein, "Fatal Beating: Settlement Seen in Rodriguez Suit," *Courier Post*, October 3, 1975, 3.

24. Each articulation of these times points out the loss of commercial retail and the economic assessment of harm and damage to Camden's future. "In the years after the riots, virtually every major retailer on Broadway—which once boasted J. C. Penney's, Woolworths, and Lit Brothers—left town. Before the advent of malls, Camden had been the shopping destina-

tion for South Jersey residents." In the wake of Camden's transformation what emerges is another site-specific commerce, corner markets and today the downtown business of complex medical care. In 1968, Camden city's riot insurance lapsed; the city itself became for a time, uninsurable, as the Insurance Company of North America refused to renew Camden's riot and civil disobedience coverage. "Camden's Riot Insurance Lapses," *Courier Post*, August 1, 1968, 7. See also "In Camden, a Bit of the Old Bustle," *Philadelphia Inquirer*, August 4, 1991, 19.

Chapter One. Toward Camden

Epigraph: Fred Moten, "B 4," *Poetry Magazine*, February 6, 2010, https://www.poetryfoundation.org/harriet/2010/02/b-4.

1. Mom texts me: "The letter Dad wrote from Vietnam is dated January 22, 1968. That's his birthday! I just realized that! Things became bad throughout the year, when he and his buddies were bathing in a river and they started to get hit, bombs, and Dad got hit on his left leg, by the knee. He got out of the water and hopped into a 'hole' with other guys. That was when he was wounded and sent to Japan to recuperate. When he came back, he found out that many of the guys in his unit had been killed. That bombed him out. That affected him so much that he kind of changed inside. Even now Dad remembers every detail. One good thing he did was help people, help the older ladies and poor people. He would get things for them and learned to communicate with them in their own language. He has stories to tell. He wrote letters to me. I did not receive all of them. I mailed a letter every morning to him. He would get them in bunches sometimes, as the company moved frequently. Will call you tomorrow morning, Lord willing. [Kiss emoji]"

2. Atul Gawande, "The Hot Spotters," *New Yorker*, January 24, 2011.

3. David Weisburd and Cody W. Telep, "Hot Spots Policing: What We Know and What We Need to Know," *Journal of Contemporary Criminal Justice* 30, no. 2 (2014): 200–220.

4. Nadine Ehlers and Shiloh Krupar, "'When Treating Patients like Criminals Makes Sense': Medical Hot Spotting, Race, and Debt," in *Subprime Health: Debt and Race in U.S. Medicine*, ed. Nadine Ehlers and Leslie R. Hinkson (Minneapolis: University of Minnesota Press, 2017), 31–54.

5. Andy McNeil, "Police Step Up Presence at Northgate," *Courier Post*, January 12, 2014, https://www.courierpostonline.com/story/news/2014/01/12/police-step-up-presence-at-northgate-i-/4437911/.

Epigraph: John Keats, "Ode on a Grecian Urn," Poetry Foundation, https://www.poetryfoundation.org/poems/44477/ode-on-a-grecian-urn.

1. "Camden, New Jersey, Mischief Night 1991: October 30 & 31, 1991—The Official Report," DVRBS.com, http://www.dvrbs.com/fire/CamdenNJ-MN-1991-OR.htm/.

2. In the "Open Letter to All Personnel Involved with the CFD on Mischief Night 1991" and "The Mischief Night October 30, 1991 Comprehensive Summary Report," which document and map the arson on Mischief Night 1991, are hot zones, spots that are recognized for homicide and drug traffic. In preparation for and in case of future fires, firefighters are warned that in these areas they might face other forms of violence. They might get assaulted or shot.

3. Henri Lefebvre asks: "If space embodies social relationships, how and why does it do so? And what relationships are they?" Henri Lefebvre, *The Production of Space*, trans. Donald Nicholson-Smith (Malden, MA: Blackwell, 1991), 27. See also Bill McGraw, "Life in the Ruins of Detroit," *History Workshop Journal*, no. 63 (spring 2007): 288–302. McGraw writes: "Abandoned homes were the kindling that fueled Detroit's notorious arson outbreaks on 30 October, the night before Halloween and a traditional evening for mischief known for decades as Devil's Night. But between the early 1980s and early 1990s, the mischief turned serious as arsonists set hundreds of fires in vacant structures, and the retrenched fire department was overwhelmed attempting to respond" (295).

4. Jerry Gray, "Camden Braces for Mischief Night Fires," *New York Times*, October 25, 1992, www.nytimes.com/1992/10/25/nyregion/camden-braces-for-mischief-night-fires.html/.

5. The visual field of poverty and the value of the inner-city poor sit squarely within view and reach of American wars of destruction and capital reinvestment. Doyle wrote (on the now defunct website) poetofpoverty.com: "Baghdad will have a new infrastructure before Camden." For more of Michael Doyle's writing see his beautiful collection of letters, Michael J. Doyle, *It's a Terrible Day: Thanks Be to God* (Camden, NJ: The Heart of Camden, Inc., 2003) and the 2008 documentary "Poet of Poverty," directed by Sean Dougherty, Tana Ross, and Freke Vuijst. In a letter dated May 1998, Michael Doyle reflects on his acquittal as one of the "Camden 28," a group of pacifists and antiwar activists who raided a draft board during the Vietnam War. He writes: "But no twist more interesting or turn more enjoyable than the (almost) four-month trial of the 'Camden 28.' I was focused on the issue that still haunts me. How could a country spend so much on the weap-

ons of war and let a Camden continue to be a place of destruction for many of its children? I had shown slides in the courtroom of war-ravaged Vietnam interspersed with slides of dilapidated buildings in Camden. Camden is a casualty of a war economy. I said then, and it still is. Why is so much of our taxes used to make weapons we do not need, and not to rebuild our inner cities with good houses that we do?" Doyle, *It's a Terrible Day*, 188.

6. "A Path Forward for Camden," Report Commissioned by the Annie E. Casey Foundation for the City of Camden and Its Constituents, June 13, 2001, available from cnjg.org. According to the 2010 census, Camden city is 48.1 percent Black and 47 percent persons of Latino or Hispanic origin; 36.1 percent of people are living below the poverty level.

7. The 2019 census data estimates Camden's population at 73,562, a median household income of $27,070 between 2014 and 2019, and a per capita income of $14,747. The percentage of people living in poverty in 2019 was estimated at 36.8 percent. "QuickFacts: Camden City, New Jersey," US Census Bureau, https://www.census.gov/quickfacts/camdencitynewjersey/, accessed August 15, 2020.

8. Gray, "Camden Braces for Mischief Night Fires."

9. Howard Gillette Jr., *Camden after the Fall: Decline and Renewal in a Post-Industrial City* (Philadelphia: University of Pennsylvania Press, 2005), 11.

10. Gillette, *Camden after the Fall*, 11; my emphasis.

11. Taylor writes: "Embodied performance, then, makes visible an entire spectrum of attitudes and values. The multi-codedness of these practices transmits as many layers of meaning as there are spectators, participants, and witnesses." Diana Taylor, *The Archive and the Repertoire* (Durham, NC: Duke University Press, 2003), 24.

12. J. B. Jackson characterizes the street as a "system of arteries," as a telling and orienting blood channel, "as a means of movement and communication and of orientation." John Brinckerhoff Jackson, *The Necessity for Ruins and Other Topics* (Amherst, MA: University of Massachusetts Press, 1980), 55.

13. See Danielle Goldman, *I Want to Be Ready: Improvised Dance as a Practice of Freedom* (Ann Arbor: University of Michigan Press, 2010). Henri Lefebvre writes: "When codes worked up from literary texts are applied to spaces—to urban spaces, say—we remain, as may be easily shown, on the purely descriptive level. Any attempt to use such codes as a means of deciphering social space must surely reduce that space itself to the status of a *message*, and the inhabiting of it to the status of a *reading*. This is to evade both history and practice." Lefebvre, *The Production of Space*, 7; my emphasis.

14. André Lepecki, "Stumble Dance," *Women and Performance: A Journal of Feminist Theory* 14, no. 1 (2004): 47–61; and André Lepecki, *Exhausting Dance*, 49.

15. "The struggle that is being waged in the Cramer Hill section epitomizes many of the topics at the center of the hotly contested property rights arena in the United States. How is 'public use' defined? Is it appropriate to transfer condemned private property to other private entities for development? Can urban redevelopment projects be racially and economically discriminatory or violate individual and civil rights? These are among the serious questions pending before the highest court in the land, and decisions in those cases have the potential to drastically alter the face of private property rights in the United States." Taylor Ruilova, "Camden 2015: Can Condemnation Power and Urban Redevelopment Plans Bring Life Back to the City?" *Rutgers Journal of Law and Urban Policy* 3, no. 3 (2006): 469.

16. Grassroots neighborhood organization and protest ultimately led to a successful 2006 lawsuit that collapsed the public/private partnership between the city of Camden and Cherokee Investments. See the Cramer Hill Development Corporation website for a description of conflicting community and corporate interest: http://cramerhillcdc.blogspot.com/. Taylor Ruilova, "Camden 2015," notes that the plan included "moving approximately 987 households, with roughly 300 homeowners and the remaining 687 residents occupying subsidized and unsubsidized rental properties and a public housing project" (258).

17. Cherokee Investment Partners deployed the word *Cherokee* as a claim to land that was not invested in Native sovereignty or contemporary Native communities, but rather as an idiom of redevelopment. "No Cherokee" signs may always signify on the histories of Indian removal and anti-Indian sentiment. However, the placement of these signs in Cramer Hill windows also and importantly conjured a Cramer Hill community that knew this "Cherokee" was a corporate entity and a rhetorical move, a name that bore no ethical or political commitment to indigenous pasts, futures, or peoplehood. I am grateful to Yomaira Figueroa and Patricia Penn Hilden for each furthering my thinking on the resonance of Cherokee in this instance.

18. Jill Bennett, *Empathic Vision: Affect, Trauma, and Contemporary Art* (Palo Alto, CA: Stanford University Press, 2005), 65.

19. Zaire Dinzey-Flores, "Temporary Housing, Permanent Communities: Public Housing Policy and Design in Puerto Rico," *Journal of Urban History* 33, no. 3 (March 2007): 467–92.

20. Walt Whitman, "I Dreamed in a Dream," in *Leaves of Grass*, https://whitmanarchive.org/published/LG/figures/ppp.00473.141.jpg/.

21. On the tension between art photography and photojournalism, see Sibylle Fischer, "Haiti: Fantasies of Bare Life," *Small Axe* 2 (June 2007): 1–15. Also see "Representations of the Erased," interview between Natascha Sadr Haghighian and Ashley Hunt: "Maps are generally too totalizing, proposing

full knowledge and discouraging more critical and creative thought. A good map, on the other hand, folds in on itself, betrays you, and reveals itself as a construction—including most of all the point of view from which it organizes and produces a visual field" (8). http://correctionsproject.com/art/writing/HUNT_HAGHIGHIAN.pdf.

22. On the gardener/set designer: "How are people going to move through the space? How is it going to make you feel? It's not just a matter of space; it's a matter of speed. You need to be slowed down a bit sometimes; things need to distract you, involve you, take you out of yourself. Obviously it is a luxury to have a garden designed for you. But I have noticed that if you are rich, designers often inflict richness on you. I have always understood that a rich person who commissions a garden from me might need other things—freedom, simplicity, calm, for example." Patrick Kinmonth, "A Sense of Place," *Vogue*, July 2010, 138.

23. The language of the frontier, at the precipice of empire, is fitting. Fassi discusses urban explorers: "Today's urban explorers resist a narrow-minded conception of city life and urban landscapes. They are among the few who contribute to the visibility of postindustrial landscapes and, by extension, the visual history of deindustrialization. However, urban explorers also describe industrial ruins according to picturesque principles." Anthony J. Fassi, "Industrial Ruins, Urban Exploring, and the Postcolonial Picturesque," *CR: The New Centennial Review* 10, no. 1 (spring 2010): 148–49.

24. Theodor Adorno writes: "The body's habituation to walking as normal stems from the good old days. It was the bourgeois form of locomotion: physical demythologization, free of the spell of hieratic pacing, roofless wandering, breathless flight. Human dignity insisted on the right to walk, a rhythm not extorted from the body by command or terror." Adorno, *Minima Moralia*, 162.

25. Paul Carter, *The Lie of the Land* (London: Faber and Faber, 1996), 4.

26. Wahneema Lubiano, "If I Could Talk about It, This Is Not What I Would Say," in "Violence, Space," special issue, *Assemblages: A Journal of Architecture and Design Culture*, no. 20 (April 1993): 56.

27. *Philadelphia Record, Scrap Drives*, 1942–43, Historical Society of Pennsylvania.

28. A focus on abundant forms of life, environmental storytelling, and slow violence builds on the scholarship of geographer Clyde Woods and literary scholar Rob Nixon.

29. Anthony Fassi writes: "The images urban explorers make available on websites and blogs function as public archives of a rapidly disappearing built environment. As more parts of our cities and their former sites of industrial production fall victim to the bulldozer and the wrecking ball, I imagine that

these public, unofficial archives will prove indispensable to future analyses of industrial history. They are a valuable resource not only to those seeking an offbeat thrill, but to all of us who look for meaning among our cities' hidden recesses and the untold stories of their industrial pasts" ("Industrial Ruins," 152). The Cramer Hills Facebook group uses memory to comment on images; another level of connection and a sense of displacement fuels these commentaries. This group becomes not simply an archive of untold stories, but an ongoing story about the racialization of structural decline and social abandonment.

30. "Just as none of us is outside or beyond geography, none of us is completely free from the struggle over geography. That struggle is complex and interesting because it is not only about soldiers and cannons but also about ideas, about forms, about image and imaginings." Edward Said, *Culture and Imperialism* (New York: Vintage, 1994), 7.

31. Paul W. Kelley, Cramer Hill Memories, Photograph 297, September 27, 2010, https://www.facebook.com/groups/253824373147/.

32. Fred Moten, "Music against the Law of Reading the Future and 'Rodney King,'" in "The Future of the Profession," special edition, *Journal of the Midwest Modern Language Association* 27, no. 1 (spring 1994): 56.

33. Robert Beauregard, quoted in Gillette, *Camden after the Fall*, 61.

34. See Tim Edesor et al., "Playing in Industrial Ruins: Interrogating Teleological Understandings of Play in Spaces of Material Alterity and Low Surveillances," in *Urban Wildscapes*, ed. Anna Jorgensen and Richard Keenan (London: Routledge, 2012), 65–77.

35. "Homi Bhabha has said, 'The globe shrinks for those who own it; for the displaced or the dispossessed, the migrant or refugee, no distance is more awesome than the few feet across borders or frontiers.' Today's site-oriented practices inherit the task of demarcating the relational specificity that can hold in tension the distant poles of spatial experiences described by Bhabha. This means addressing the differences of adjacencies and distances between one thing, one person, one place, one thought, one fragment next to another, rather than invoking equivalencies via one thing after another. Only those cultural practices that have this relational sensibility can turn local encounters into long-term commitments and transform passing intimacies into indelible, unretractable social marks so that the sequence of sites that we inhabit in our life's traversal does not become generalized into an undifferentiated serialization, one place after another." Homi Bhabha, quoted in Miwon Kwon, "One Place after Another: Notes on Site Specificity," *October* 80 (spring 1997): 110.

36. "[Charles] Branas has found compelling evidence of a strong link be-

tween increased rates of aggravated assaults and a rise in the number of vacant lots in an urban area. By overlaying police data on aggravated assaults in particular geographic areas between 2002 and 2006 with corresponding census demographics data and vacant property records, Branas and his team of Penn researchers discovered that total assaults in a given set of blocks increased by 18.5 percent for every increase in vacancy in that area. The positive correlation was stronger for gun assaults, which increased by 22.4 percent with each new vacant lot, than for non-gun attacks, which rose by 14.8 percent for every increase in vacancy." Ariella Cohen, "Vacant Lots = Violence," NextCity.org, June 3, 2009, https://nextcity.org/daily/entry/vacant-lots-violence/.

37. David Scott, "The Re-enchantment of Humanism: An Interview with Sylvia Wynter," *Small Axe* 8 (September 2000): 164.

38. Joseph Roach notes that "performance genealogies draw on the idea of expressive movements as mnemonic reserves, including patterned movements made and remembered by bodies, residual movements retained implicitly in images or words (or in the silences between them), and imaginary movements dreamed in minds not prior to language but constitutive of it." Joseph Roach, *Cities of the Dead: Circum-Atlantic Performance* (New York: Columbia University Press, 1996), 26.

39. Adriana Cavarero writes: "This is rather an irreflexive recognition, already at work in the exhibitive nature of the self, which is rendered even more explicit in the active and desiring practice of reciprocal storytelling. The relational character of the ethic that responds is not therefore the fruit of a choice; or, rather, the object of a possible appraisal or the result of a grandiose strategy. It is rather the necessary aspect of an identity which, from beginning to end, is intertwined with other lives—with reciprocal exposures and innumerable gazes—and needs the other's tale." Adriana Cavarero, *Relating Narratives: Storytelling and Selfhood* (New York: Routledge, 2000), 88.

Chapter Three. Demolition Futures

1. Bonnie Yochelson and Daniel Czitrom, *Rediscovering Jacob Riis: Exposure Journalism and Photographs in Turn-of-the-Century New York* (Chicago: University of Chicago Press, 2008); Ben Campkin, *Remaking London: Decline and Regeneration in Urban Culture* (New York: Palgrave Macmillan, 2013).

2. Jesse Serwer, "Interview with Camilo Jose Vergara" (2007), *ASX Magazine*, November 6, 2009, http://americansuburbx.com/2009/11/interview-interview-with-camilo-jose.html.

3. "The Riverfront State Prison Site Reuse Study," https://clarkecatonhintz
.com/project/riverfront-state-prison-site-reuse-study/.

4. The cost of the Riverfront State Prison construction is estimated
at $31 million, and it housed more than one thousand people (inmates).
"Save Our Waterfront is an organization comprised of individuals who live,
work and worship in the North Camden neighborhood of Camden, New
Jersey. Founded in 1992, SOW grew out of the community's opposition to
the New Jersey Department of Corrections' plan to build a second prison in
North Camden. SOW successfully dissuaded the NJDOC from constructing
a second prison. The group serves as a coherent voice for the North Camden community and is responsible for coordinating the creation and implementation of the original North Camden Plan adopted in 1993.

"In 2006, Save Our Waterfront began updating that plan to reflect the
reuse potential of North Camden's waterfront based on the premise that
the Riverfront State Prison would be closing. That updated plan, completed
in 2009, represents the community's evolving hopes and priorities for the
future and provides an updated long-range vision for North Camden. Save
Our Waterfront is committed to the implementation of the North Camden
Neighborhood Plan. To that end, SOW hosts a monthly stakeholder meeting
to continue to harness the community's interests and momentum and has
created several subcommittees to address elements of neighborhood revitalization." "History," Save Our Waterfront website, http://www.sow-camden
.org/about/history/.

5. Monica Yant Kinney, "Camden Site's Charm Ready to Bust Out," *Philadelphia Inquirer*, August 30, 2009, https://www.inquirer.com/philly/news
/20090830_Monica_Yant_Kinney_. html.

6. Camden Redevelopment Agency, "Executive Summary," in the "North
Camden Neighborhood Plan," March 2008, 4, http://camdenredevelopment
.org/.

7. "The Riverfront State Prison Site Reuse Study," https://clarkecaton
hintz.com/project/riverfront- state- prison- site- reuse- study/.

8. Camden Redevelopment Agency, "Executive Summary," 4.

9. Fred Moten, *In the Break: The Aesthetics of the Black Radical Tradition*
(Minneapolis: University of Minnesota Press, 2003).

10. Clyde Woods, "Les Misérables of New Orleans: Trap Economics and
the Asset Stripping Blues, Part 1," in "In the Wake of Katrina: New Paradigms and Social Visions," special issue, *American Quarterly* 61, no. 3 (September 2009): 774. Woods also writes: "The institutions of racial enclosure and
impoverishment fueled the loss of human life, community stability, and economic assets. Enclosures are maintained by a system of militarized regula-
tion, physical boundaries, and social, political, and economic traps, referred

to here as trap economics. These boundaries are also defended by a representational system that provides intellectual justification for, and naturalizes, this form of social conflict" (774).

11. Ruth Wilson Gilmore, "Fatal Couplings of Power and Difference: Notes on Racism and Geography," *Professional Geographer* 54, no. 1 (2002): 16.

12. "The Department of the Treasury, on behalf of the Department of Corrections, is authorized to sell and convey to the New Jersey Economic Development Authority all of the State's right, title, and interest in and to the property known as the Riverfront State Prison, consisting of a 16 +- acre [*sic*] parcel of land and improvements situated on Block 79, Lot 13 in the City of Camden, Camden County, which has been declared surplus to the needs of the State. The consideration to be paid to the State by the authority for the sale and conveyance of the property shall be the sum of one dollar." Donald Norcross, sponsor, Senate, No. 2075, State of New Jersey, 215th Legislature, introduced June 14, 2012, "Synopsis: Authorizes Sale of Site of Former Riverfront State Prison in City of Camden as State Surplus Property to NJEDA for Public Auction to Prequalified Developer." http://www.njleg .state.nj.us/2012/Bills/S2500/2075_R1.pdf.

13. *Mega Breakdown*, episode 16, "Prison," aired May 20, 2011, on National Geographic Channel, http://natgeotv.com/asia/mega-breakdown2/about.

14. Organized by the grassroots group STOP (Stop Trauma on People) and Hopeworks 'N Camden, a youth development agency, the Trauma Summit was attended by community members and health care practitioners, including Jeffrey Brenner, the founder of Camden Coalition of Healthcare Providers. As an outcome of the Trauma Summit, this group founded Camden Healing 10 to initiate a public discussion of trauma-informed care and healing. Indeed, Hopeworks 'N Camden is in the process of becoming certified by the Sanctuary Institute. See https://hopeworks.org /about/our-history/; and Kim Mulford, "Group Hopes to Heal Camden's Deadly Stress," *Courier Post*, May 9, 2014, http://www.courierpostonline.com /story/news/local/south-jersey/2014/05/09/group-hopes-heal-camdens-deadly -stress/8929847/.

15. In 2011 Cooper's Ferry Development merged with Greater Camden Partnership to form Cooper's Ferry Partnership. The mission of Cooper's Ferry Partnership is "to establish public and private partnerships to effect sustainable economic revitalization and promote Camden as a place in which to live, to work, to visit, and to invest." Cooper's Ferry Development Association describes its mission from 1984 to 2000 as successfully concentrating on the redevelopment of Camden's downtown waterfront.

16. www.camdennightgarden.com/festivals, accessed May 30, 2015,

website now defunct. For a history of Camden Night Gardens, including the 2015 event, see http://www.ctlcamden.com/camden-night-gardens.html.

17. https://creative-nbny.squarespace.com/2015-shadow-stage, accessed May 30, 2015, website now defunct. For images and an explanation of the 2015 Camden Night Gardens and Shadow Stage, see also https://www.art placeamerica.org/funded-projects/camden-night-gardens-cng.

18. Angela Y. Davis, *Abolition Democracy: Beyond Empire, Prisons, and Torture* (New York: Seven Stories Press, 2005).

19. "Documented Middle Passage Sites in the Continental United States," Middle Passage Ceremonies and Port Markers Project: Remembering Ancestors, September 26, 2017, https://www.middlepassageproject.org/documented -sites/.

20. Leslie Marmon Silko, *Ceremony* (New York: Penguin, 2016), 108.

21. President Barack Obama, "Remarks by the President on Community Policing," May 18, 2015, https://obamawhitehouse.archives.gov/the-press -office/2015/05/18/remarks-president-community-policing.

22. Camden Redevelopment Agency, Cramer Hill Neighborhood Plan, "Cramer Hill Redevelopment Study," 50, http://camdenredevelopment.org /Plans/Plans/Redevelopment-Plan.aspx.

23. Christina Sharpe, *In the Wake: On Blackness and Being* (Durham, NC: Duke University Press, 2007), 208.

24. Benjamin Eldon Stevens, "Medea in Jesmyn Ward's *Salvage the Bones*," *International Journal of the Classical Tradition* 25, no. 2 (2018): 175.

25. "Cramer Hill Redevelopment Study," 40.

26. Woods, "Life after Death," 63.

Chapter Four. Halfway Houses

1. Eleanor Ray, "The Cellar," *The Mickle Street Review*, no. 1 (1979): 94.

2. Ray, "The Cellar," 95.

3. Walt Whitman, "I Sing the Body Electric," in *Leaves of Grass* (Norton Critical Edition), ed. Sculley Bradley and Harold W. Blodgett (New York: W. W. Norton, 1973), 96.

4. George Hutchinson, "Afterword: At Whitman's Grave," in *Whitman Noir: Black America and the Good Gray Poet*, ed. Ivy G. Wilson (Iowa City: University of Iowa Press, 2014), 179–86.

5. Gloria Anzaldúa, *Borderlands / La Frontera: The New Mestiza* (San Francisco: Aunt Lute, 2012), 100.

BIBLIOGRAPHY

/

Adorno, Theodor W. *Minima Moralia: Reflections from Damaged Life*. Translated by E. F. N. Jephcott. London: Verso, 2005.

Agamben, Giorgio. *Homo Sacer: Sovereign Power and Bare Life*. Stanford, CA: Stanford University Press, 1998.

Ahmed, Sara. *Living a Feminist Life*. Durham, NC: Duke University Press, 2018.

Alarcon, Norma. "Traddutora, Traditora: A Paradigmatic Figure of Chicana Feminism." *Cultural Critique*, no. 13 (autumn 1989): 57–87.

Alexander, M. Jacqui. *Pedagogies of Crossing: Meditations on Feminism, Sexual Politics, Memory, and the Sacred*. Durham, NC: Duke University Press, 2006.

Anzaldúa, Gloria. *Borderlands / La Frontera: The New Mestiza*, 4th ed. San Francisco: Aunt Lute, 2012.

Arteaga, Alfred. *House with the Blue Bed*. San Francisco: Mercury House, 1997.

Baldwin, James. *Notes of a Native Son*. Boston: Beacon Press, 2012.

Barot, Rick. "Tarp." *Poetry Magazine*, May 2013. https://www.poetryfoundation.org/poetrymagazine/poems/56241/tarp.

Bell, W. Kamau, host. *United Shades of America*. Season 1, episode 4, "Protect and Serve?" Aired May 15, 2016, on CNN.

Benjamin, Walter. *The Arcades Project*. Translated by Howard Eiland and Kevin McLaughlin. Cambridge, MA: Harvard University Press, 1999.

Benjamin, Walter. *Illuminations*. Edited by Hannah Arendt. New York: Schocken, 1968.

Bennett, Jill. *Empathic Vision: Affect, Trauma, and Contemporary Art*. Palo Alto, CA: Stanford University Press, 2005.

Biehl, João. *Vita: Life in a Zone of Social Abandonment*. Berkeley: University of California Press, 2005.

Brooks, Gwendolyn. *Maud Martha*. Chicago: Third World Press, 1993.

Brown, Jayna. *Babylon Girls: Black Women Performers and the Shaping of the Modern*. Durham, NC: Duke University Press, 2008.

Brown, Simone. *Dark Matters: On the Surveillance of Blackness*. Durham, NC: Duke University Press, 2015.

Butler, Judith. *Frames of War: When Is Life Grievable?* London: Verso, 2010.

Cacho, Lisa Marie. *Social Death: Racialized Rightlessness and the Criminalization of the Unprotected*. New York: New York University Press, 2012.

Calvino, Italo. *Invisible Cities*. Translated by William Weaver. San Diego: Harcourt, 1974.

Camp, Jordan T. "Blues Geographies and the Security Turn: Interpreting the Housing Crisis in Los Angeles." *American Quarterly* 64, no. 3 (2012): 543–70.

Campkin, Ben. *Remaking London: Decline and Regeneration in Urban Culture*. New York: Palgrave Macmillan, 2013.

Carter, Paul. *The Lie of the Land*. London: Faber and Faber, 1996.

Cavarero, Adriana. *Relating Narratives: Storytelling and Selfhood*. New York: Routledge, 2000.

Cervenak, Sarah Jane. *Wandering: Philosophical Performances of Racial and Sexual Freedom*. Durham, NC: Duke University Press, 2014.

Cheng, Anne Anlin. *The Melancholy of Race*. Oxford: Oxford University Press, 2001.

"Connect the Lots Camden." City of Camden and Cooper's Ferry Partnership. http://www.ctlcamden.com/camden-night-gardens.html.

Cowie, Jefferson. *Capital Moves: RCA's Seventy-Year Quest for Cheap Labor*. New York: New Press, 2001.

"Cramer Hill Redevelopment Study." Camden Redevelopment Agency, Cramer Hill Neighborhood Plan, 50. http://camdenredevelopment.org/Plans/Plans/Redevelopment-Plan.aspx.

Crenshaw, Kimberle. "Mapping the Margins: Intersectionality, Identity Politics, and Violence against Women of Color." *Stanford Law Review* 43, no. 6 (July 1991): 1241–99.

Davis, Angela Y. *Abolition Democracy: Beyond Empire, Prisons, and Torture*. New York: Seven Stories Press, 2005.

Davis, Angela Y. *Are Prisons Obsolete?* New York: Seven Stories Press, 2003.

Davis, Mike. *City of Quartz: Excavating the Future of Los Angeles*. New York: Vintage, 1992.

Dayan, Colin. *The Law Is a White Dog: How Legal Rituals Make and Unmake Persons*. Princeton, NJ: Princeton University Press, 2013.

De Certeau, Michel. *The Practice of Everyday Life*. Translated by Steven Randall. Berkeley: University of California Press, 1984.

Delaney, Samuel. *Times Square Red, Times Square Blue*. New York: New York University Press, 1999.

Deleuze, Gilles, and Félix Guattari. *Anti-Oedipus: Capitalism and Schizophrenia*. Translated by Robert Hurley. Minneapolis: University of Minnesota Press, 1983.

Derrida, Jacques. *Archive Fever: A Freudian Impression*. Translated by Eric Prenowitz. Chicago: University of Chicago Press, 1998.

Desmond, Matthew. *Evicted: Poverty and Profit in the American City*. New York: Penguin, 2016.

Diamond, Elin. *Unmaking Mimesis: Essays on Feminism and Theatre*. New York: Routledge, 1997.

Dinzey-Flores, Zaire. "Temporary Housing, Permanent Communities: Public Housing Policy and Design in Puerto Rico." *Journal of Urban History* 33, no. 3 (March 2007): 467–92.

"Documented Middle Passage Sites in the Continental United States." Middle Passage Ceremonies and Port Makers Project: Remembering Ancestors. September 26, 2017. www.middlepassageproject.org/wp-content/uploads/2017/09/mp_by_action_9_26_2017.pdf.

Doyle, Michael J. *It's a Terrible Day . . . Thanks Be to God*. Camden, NJ: The Heart of Camden Inc., 2003.

Du Bois, W. E. B. *The Souls of Black Folk*. New York: Penguin, 1989.

Edesor, Tim, Bethan Evans, Julian Holloway, Steve Millington, and Jon Binnie. "Playing in Industrial Ruins: Interrogating Teleological Understandings of Play in Spaces of Material Alterity and Low Surveillances." In *Urban Wildscapes*, edited by Anna Jorgensen and Richard Keenan, 65–79. London: Routledge, 2012.

Edwards, Brent Hayes. *The Practice of Diaspora: Literature, Translation, and the Rise of Black Internationalism*. Cambridge, MA: Harvard University Press, 2003.

Ehlers, Nadine, and Shiloh Krupar. "'When Treating Patients Like Criminals Makes Sense': Medical Hot Spotting, Race, and Debt." In *Subprime Health: Debt and Race in U.S. Medicine*, edited by Nadine Ehlers and Leslie R. Hinkson, 31–54. Minneapolis: University of Minnesota Press, 2017.

Espada, Martín. *City of Coughing and Dead Radiators*. New York: W. W. Norton, 1993.

Espada, Martín. *Rebellion Is the Circle of a Lover's Hands*. Translated by Camilo

Pérez-Bustillo and Martín Espada. Willimantic, CT: Curbstone Press, 1990.

"Executive Summary." Camden Redevelopment Agency's North Camden Neighborhood Plan, March 2008, 4. http://camdenredevelopment.org/.

Fabian, Johannes. *Memory against Culture: Arguments and Reminders*. Durham, NC: Duke University Press, 2007.

Fassi, Anthony J. "Industrial Ruins, Urban Exploring, and the Postcolonial Picturesque." *CR: The New Centennial Review* 10, no. 1 (spring 2010): 141–52.

Ferreira da Silva, Denise. "No-Bodies: Law, Raciality and Violence." *Meritum (Belo Horizate)* 9, no. 1 (2014): 119–62.

Fischer, Sibylle. "Haiti: Fantasies of Bare Life." *Small Axe* 2 (June 2007): 1–15.

Foucault, Michel. *Discipline and Punish: The Birth of the Prison*. New York: Pantheon, 1977.

Fuentes, Marisa J. *Dispossessed Lives: Enslaved Women, Violence, and the Archive*. Philadelphia: University of Pennsylvania Press, 2016.

Fullilove, Mindy. *Root Shock: How Tearing Up City Neighborhoods Hurts America, and What We Can Do about It*. New York: One World/Ballantine, 2004.

Fullilove, Mindy. *Urban Alchemy: Restoring Joy in America's Sorted Out Cities*. New York: New Village Press, 2013.

Gil, José. *Metamorphosis of the Body*. Translated by Stephen Muecke. Minneapolis: University of Minnesota Press, 1998.

Gillette, Howard, Jr. *Camden after the Fall: Decline and Renewal in a Post-Industrial City*. Philadelphia: University of Pennsylvania Press, 2005.

Gilmore, Ruth Wilson. "Fatal Couplings of Power and Difference: Notes on Racism and Geography." *Professional Geographer* 54, no. 1 (2002): 15–24.

Gilmore, Ruth Wilson. *Golden Gulag: Prisons, Surplus, Crisis, and Opposition in Globalizing California*. Berkeley: University of California Press, 2007.

Gilroy, Paul. *The Black Atlantic: Modernity and Double Consciousness*. Cambridge, MA: Harvard University Press, 1993.

Glissant, Édouard. *Poetics of Relation*. Translated by Betsy Wing. Ann Arbor: University of Michigan Press, 1997.

Goldberger, Paul. *Why Architecture Matters*. New Haven, CT: Yale University Press, 2009.

Goldman, Danielle. *I Want to Be Ready: Improvised Dance as a Practice of Freedom*. Ann Arbor: University of Michigan Press, 2010.

Gordon, Avery F. *Ghostly Matters: Haunting and the Sociological Imagination*. Minneapolis: University of Minnesota Press, 1997.

Gray, Jerry. "Camden Braces for Mischief Night Fires." *New York Times*, October 25, 1992. www.nytimes/1992/10/25/nyregion/camden-braces-for-mischief-night-fires.html.

Harney, Stefano, and Fred Moten. *The Undercommons: Fugitive Planning and Black Study*. Brooklyn, NY: Minor Compositions, 2013.

Harper, Phillip Brian. "The Evidence of Felt Intuition: Minority Experience, Everyday Life, and Critical Speculative Knowledge." *GLQ: A Journal of Lesbian and Gay Studies* 6, no. 4 (2000): 641–57.

Hartman, Saidiya. *Lose Your Mother: A Journey along the Atlantic Slave Route*. New York: Farrar, Straus and Giroux, 2007.

Hartman, Saidiya V. *Scenes of Subjection: Terror, Slavery, and Self-Making in Nineteenth-Century America*. New York: Oxford University Press, 1997.

Harvey, David. *Social Justice and the City*. Rev. ed. Athens: University of Georgia Press, 2009.

Hilden, Patricia Penn. *When Nickels Were Indians*. Smithsonian Series in Native American Literatures. Washington, DC: Smithsonian, 1995.

Holland, Sharon. *Raising the Dead: Readings of Death and (Black) Subjectivity*. Durham, NC: Duke University Press, 2000.

Holloway, Karla. *Private Bodies, Public Texts: Race, Gender, and a Cultural Bioethics*. Durham, NC: Duke University Press, 2011.

Hutchinson, George. "Afterword: At Whitman's Grave." In *Whitman Noir: Black America and the Good Gray Poet*, edited by Ivy G. Wilson, 179–86. Iowa City: University of Iowa Press, 2014.

Invincible Cities. United States, 2006. Web Archive. https://www.loc.gov/item/lcwaN0012600/.

Jackson, John Brinckerhoff. *Discovering the Vernacular Landscape*. New Haven, CT: Yale University Press, 1984.

Jackson, John Brinckerhoff. *The Necessity for Ruins and Other Topics*. Amherst, MA: University of Massachusetts Press, 1980.

James, Joy. *Resisting State Violence: Radicalism, Gender, and Race in U.S. Culture*. Minneapolis: University of Minnesota Press, 1996.

Jenkins, Candice. *Private Lives, Proper Relations: Regulating Black Intimacy*. Minneapolis: University of Minnesota Press, 2007.

Johnson, Gaye Theresa. *Spaces of Conflict, Sounds of Solidarity: Music, Race, and Spatial Entitlement in Los Angeles*. Berkeley: University of California Press, 2013.

Keats, John. "Ode on a Grecian Urn." In *John Keats: Selected Poems*. London: Penguin, 2007.

Kelley, Robin D. G. *Race Rebels: Culture, Politics, and the Black Working Class*. New York: Free Press, 1994.

King, Jason. "Which Way Is Down? Improvisations on Black Mobility." *Women and Performance: A Journal of Feminist Theory* 14, no. 1 (2004): 25–45.

Kinney, Monica Yant. "Camden Site's Charm Ready to Bust Out." *Philadelphia Inquirer*, August 30, 2009. Accessed May 2015. https://www.inquirer.com/philly/news/20090830_Monica_Yant_Kinney_.html.

Kwon, Miwon. "One Place after Another: Notes on Site Specificity." *October* 80 (spring 1997): 85–110.

Lefebvre, Henri. *The Production of Space*. Translated by Donald Nicholson-Smith. Malden, MA: Blackwell, 1991.

Lepecki, André. *Exhausting Dance: Performance and the Politics of Movement*. New York: Routledge, 2006.

Lepecki, André. "Stumble Dance." *Women and Performance: A Journal of Feminist Theory* 14, no. 1 (2004): 47–61.

Levins Morales, Aurora. *Kindling: Writings on the Body*. Cambridge, MA: Palabrera Press, 2013.

Lipsitz, George. *How Racism Takes Place*. Philadelphia: Temple University Press, 2011.

Lorde, Audre. *The Cancer Journals: Special Edition*. San Francisco: Aunt Lute, 2006.

Lubiano, Wahneema. *The House That Race Built: Original Essays by Toni Morrison, Angela Y. Davis, Cornel West, and Others on Black Americans and Politics in America Today*. New York: Vintage, 1998.

Lubiano, Wahneema. "If I Could Talk about It, This Is Not What I Would Say." In "Violence, Space," special issue, *Assemblages: A Journal of Architecture and Design Culture*, no. 20 (April 1993): 56–57.

Lugones, Maria. *Pilgrimages/Peregrinajes: Theorizing Coalition against Multiple Oppressions*. New York: Rowan, Littlefield, 2003.

Manalansan, Martin F., IV. "Race, Violence, and Neoliberal Spatial Politics in the Global City." *Social Text* 23, nos. 3–4 (fall–winter 2005): 141–55.

Manalansan, Martin F., IV. "The 'Stuff' of Archives: Mess, Migration, and Queer Lives." *Radical History Review* 2014, no. 120 (fall 2014): 94–107.

Manning, Erin. *The Minor Gesture*. Durham, NC: Duke University Press, 2016.

Massey, Douglas S., and Nancy A. Denton. *American Apartheid: Segregation and the Making of the Underclass*. Cambridge, MA: Harvard University Press, 1993.

McDowell, Linda. *Gender, Identity and Place: Understanding Feminist Geographies*. Illustrated ed. Minneapolis: University of Minnesota Press, 1999.

McGraw, Bill. "Life in the Ruins of Detroit." *History Workshop Journal*, no. 63 (spring 2007): 288–302.

McKittrick, Katherine. *Demonic Grounds: Black Women and the Cartographies of Struggle*. Minneapolis: University of Minnesota Press, 2006.

McKittrick, Katherine. "Plantation Futures." *Small Axe: A Journal of Caribbean Criticism* 17, no. 3 (2013): 1–15.

Mega Breakdown. Episode 16, "Prison." Aired May 20, 2011, on National Geographic Channel. Accessed May 2015. http://natgeotv.com/asia/mega-breakdown2/about.

Moore, Darnell L. *No Ashes in the Fire: Coming of Age Black and Free in America*. New York: Nation Books, 2018.

Moran, D., and Y. Jewkes. "'Green' Prisons: Rethinking the 'Sustainability' of the Carceral Estate." *Geographica Helvetica* 69 (2014): 345–53.

Morrison, Toni. "The Site of Memory." In *Out There: Marginalization and Contemporary Culture*, reprint ed., edited by Russell Ferguson, Martha Gever, Trinh T. Minh-ha, Cornel West, and Félix Gonzáles-Torres, 299–324. Cambridge, MA: MIT Press, 1992.

Moten, Fred. "B 4." *Poetry Magazine*, February 6, 2010. https://www.poetry foundation.org/harriet/2010/02/b-4.

Moten, Fred. *In the Break: The Aesthetics of the Black Radical Tradition*. Minneapolis: University of Minnesota Press, 2003.

Moten, Fred. "Music against the Law of Reading the Future and 'Rodney King.'" In "The Future of the Profession," special edition, *Journal of the Midwest Modern Language Association* 27, no. 1 (spring 1994): 51–64.

Muñoz, Carlos, Jr. *Youth, Identity, Power: The Chicano Movement*. Revised and expanded ed. London: Verso, 2007.

Nixon, Rob. *Slow Violence and the Environmentalism of the Poor*. Cambridge, MA: Harvard University Press, 2013.

Norcross, Donald, sponsor. Senate, No. 2075, State of New Jersey, 215th Legislature. Introduced June 14, 2012. "Synopsis: Authorizes Sale of Site of Former Riverfront State Prison in City of Camden as State Surplus Property to NJEDA for Public Auction to Prequalified Developer." http://www.njleg.state.nj.us/2012/Bills/S2500/2075_R1.pdf.

Obama, Barack. "Remarks by the President on Community Policing." The White House Office of the Press Secretary website, May 18, 2015. https://obamawhitehouse.archives.gov/the-press-office/2015/05/18/remarks-president-community-policing.

Omi, Michael, and Howard Winant. *Racial Formation in the United States*. 3rd ed. New York: Routledge, 2015.

"A Path Forward for Camden." Report Commissioned by the Annie E. Casey Foundation for the City of Camden and Its Constituents. June 13, 2001. Available from cnjg.org.

Penn, Kenneth L. "Open Letter to All Personnel Involved with the CFD on Mischief Night." City of Camden Mischief Night, October 30,

1991. Camden Fire Department Report. http://www.dvrbs.com/fire /CamdenNJ-MN-1991-OR.htm.

Phelan, Peggy. *Mourning Sex: Performing Public Memories*. London: Routledge, 1997.

Rankine, Claudia. *Citizen: An American Epic*. Minneapolis: Graywolf Press, 2014.

Rankine, Claudia. *Don't Let Me Be Lonely: An American Lyric*. Minneapolis: Graywolf Press, 2004.

Ray, Eleanor. "The Cellar." *The Mickle Street Review*, no. 1 (1979): 94.

Reynolds, David S. *Walt Whitman's America: A Cultural Biography*. New York: Vintage, 1996.

"The Riverfront State Prison Site Reuse Study." https://clarkecatonhintz.com /project/riverfront-state-prison-site-reuse-study/.

Roach, Joseph. *Cities of the Dead: Circum-Atlantic Performance*. New York: Columbia University Press, 1996.

Rodriguez, Abraham. *The Buddha Book: A Novel*. New York: Picador, 2001.

Rodriguez, Abraham, Jr. *The Boy without a Flag: Tales of the South Bronx*. 2nd rev. ed. Minneapolis: Milkweed Editions, 1999.

Rothstein, Richard. "The Making of Ferguson: Public Policy at the Root of Its Troubles." Economic Policy Institute, October 15, 2014. https://www .epi.org/publication/making-ferguson/.

Ruilova, Taylor. "Camden 2015: Can Condemnation Power and Urban Redevelopment Plans Bring Life Back to the City?" *Rutgers Journal of Law and Urban Policy* 3, no. 3 (2006): 441–70.

Said, Edward. *Culture and Imperialism*. New York: Vintage, 1994.

Saldívar, José David. *The Dialectics of Our America: Genealogy, Cultural Critique, and Literary History*. Durham, NC: Duke University Press, 2002.

Sandoval, Chela. *The Methodology of the Oppressed*. Minneapolis: University of Minnesota Press, 2000.

Sassen, Saskia. *Cities in a World Economy*. 2nd ed. New York: SAGE, 2011.

Sassen, Saskia. *Globalization and Its Discontents*. New York: New Press, 1998.

Scott, David. "The Re-enchantment of Humanism: An Interview with Sylvia Wynter." *Small Axe* 8 (September 2000): 119–207.

Serwer, Jesse. "Interview with Camilo Jose Vergara." (2007). *ASX Magazine*, November 6, 2009. http://americansuburbx.com/2009/11/interview -interview-with-camilo-jose.html.

Shabazz, Rashad. *Spatializing Blackness: Architectures of Confinement and Black Masculinity in Chicago*. Urbana: University of Illinois Press, 2015.

Shakur, Assata. *Assata: An Autobiography*. Westport, CT: Lawrence Hill, 2001.

Sharpe, Christina. *In the Wake: On Blackness and Being*. Durham, NC: Duke University Press, 2007.

Silko, Leslie Marmon. *Ceremony*. New York: Penguin, 2016.

Smith, Bruce. *Shakespeare/Cut: Rethinking Cutwork in an Age of Distraction*. London: Oxford University Press, 2016.

Spade, Dean. *Normal Life: Administrative Violence, Critical Trans Politics, and the Limits of Law*. Durham, NC: Duke University Press, 2015.

Spillers, Hortense. *Black, White, and in Color: Essays on American Literature and Culture*. Chicago: University of Chicago Press, 2003.

Stevens, Benjamin Eldon. "Medea in Jesmyn Ward's *Salvage the Bones*." *International Journal of the Classic Tradition* 25, no. 2 (2018): 158–77.

Stevenson, Lisa. *Life Beside Itself: Imagining Care in the Canadian Arctic*. Oakland: University of California Press, 2014.

Stewart, Kathleen. *Ordinary Affects*. Durham, NC: Duke University Press, 2007.

Tang, Eric. *Unsettled: Cambodian Refugees in the NYC Hyperghetto*. Philadelphia: Temple University Press, 2015.

Taylor, Diana. *The Archive and the Repertoire*. Durham, NC: Duke University Press, 2003.

Thomas, Deborah. *Exceptional Violence*. Durham, NC: Duke University Press, 2011.

Tretheway, Natasha. *Beyond Katrina: A Meditation on the Mississippi Gulf Coast*. Athens: University of Georgia Press, 2012.

Trouillot, Michel-Rolph. *Silencing the Past: Power and the Production of History*. Boston: Beacon Press, 1995.

Tsing, Anna. *The Mushroom at the End of the World: On the Possibility of Life in Capitalist Ruins*. Princeton, NJ: Princeton University Press, 2017.

Tuan, Yi-Fu. *Space and Place: The Perspective of Experience*. Minneapolis: University of Minnesota Press, 2001.

Venkatesh, Sudhir Alladi. *American Project: The Rise and Fall of a Modern Ghetto*. Cambridge, MA: Harvard University Press, 2000.

Venkatesh, Sudhir Alladi. *Off the Books: The Underground Economy of the Urban Poor*. Cambridge, MA: Harvard University Press, 2009.

Vergara, Camilo José. *American Ruins*. New York: Monacelli Press, 1999.

Wacquant, Loïc. *Prisons of Poverty*. Minneapolis: University of Minnesota Press, 2009.

Wacquant, Loïc. *Punishing the Poor: The Neoliberal Government of Social Insecurity*. Durham, NC: Duke University Press, 2009.

Wallschlaeger, Nicki. *Houses*. Providence, RI: Horse Less Press, 2015.

Ward, Jesmyn. *Men We Reaped: A Memoir*. New York: Bloomsbury, 2014.

Weeks, Kathi. "'Hours for What We Will': Work, Family, and the Movement for Shorter Hours." *Feminist Studies* 35, no. 1 (spring 2009): 101–27.

Weisburd, David, and Cody W. Telep. "Hot Spots Policing: What We Know and What We Need to Know." *Journal of Contemporary Criminal Justice* 30, no. 2 (2014): 200–220.

Weizman, Eyal. *Hollow Land: Israel's Architecture of Occupation*. London: Verso, 2012.

Whitman, Walt. *Leaves of Grass* (Norton Critical Edition). Edited by Sculley Bradley and Harold W. Blodgett. New York: W. W. Norton, 1973.

Williams, William Carlos. *Paterson*. Revised ed. prepared by Christopher MacGowan. New York: New Directions, 1995.

Williamson, Terrion. *Scandalize My Name: Black Feminist Practice and the Making of Black Social Life*. New York: Fordham University Press, 2017.

Woods, Clyde. "Les Misérables of New Orleans: Trap Economics and the Asset Stripping Blues, Part 1." In "In the Wake of Katrina: New Paradigms and Social Visions," special issue. *American Quarterly* 61, no. 3 (September 2009): 769–96.

Woods, Clyde. "Life after Death." *The Professional Geographer* 54, no. 1 (2002): 62–66.

Wool, Zoë H. *After War: The Weight of Life at Walter Reed*. Durham, NC: Duke University Press, 2015.

Wynter, Sylvia. "Beyond Miranda's Meanings: Un/Silencing the 'Demonic Ground' of Caliban's Woman." In *Out of the Kumbla: Caribbean Women and Literature*, edited by Carole Boyce Davies and Elaine Savory Fido, 355–72. Trenton, NJ: Africa World Press, 1994.

Wynter, Sylvia. "The Ceremony Must Be Found: After Humanism." *boundary 2* 12, no. 3, and 13, no. 1 (spring–autumn 1984): 19–70.

Yochelson, Bonnie, and Daniel Czitrom. *Rediscovering Jacob Riis: Exposure Journalism and Photographs in Turn-of-the-Century New York*. Chicago: University of Chicago Press, 2008.

INDEX